Japan Today

In a new edition of his introductory survey of contemporary Japan, Roger Buckley traces the nation's history from its surrender in August 1945 to the present day. The revised edition, which has been rewritten to take account of Japan's changing fortunes in the 1990s, describes the recent setbacks in its economic and financial sectors and examines the major shifts in the political sphere. Despite the current challenges to Japan's prosperity, this is a remarkable story of post-war resurgence, material progress and social stability.

ROGER BUCKLEY is Professor of the History of International Relations at the International Christian University, Tokyo. His previous publications include *Occupation Diplomacy: Britain, the United States and Japan, 1945–1952* (1982), *US-Japan Alliance Diplomacy, 1945–1990* (1992) and *Hong Kong: The Road to 1997* (1997).

Japan Today

THIRD EDITION

Roger Buckley

CAMBRIDGE
UNIVERSITY PRESS

PUBLISHED BY THE PRESS SYNDICATE OF THE UNIVERSITY OF CAMBRIDGE
The Pitt Building, Trumpington Street, Cambridge CB2 1RP,
United Kingdom

CAMBRIDGE UNIVERSITY PRESS
The Edinburgh Building, Cambridge, CB2 2RU, UK
http://www.cup.cam.ac.uk
40 West 20th Street, New York, NY 10011-4211, USA
http://www.cup.org
10 Stamford Road, Oakleigh, Melbourne 3166, Australia

First published 1985
Reprinted 1987, 1988, 1989
Second edition first published 1990
Reprinted 1990, 1991, 1992, 1994, 1995, 1998

Printed in the United Kingdom at the University Press, Cambridge

Typeset in 10.5pt/15pt Swift regular

A catalogue record for this book is available from the British Library

Library of Congress Cataloguing in Publication data
Buckley, Roger, 1944–
Japan today / Roger Buckley. – 3rd ed.
p. cm.
Includes bibliographical references and index.
ISBN 0 521 64373 2 (hardback). – ISBN 0 521 64375 9 (paperback)
1. Japan – History – 1945– I. Title
DS889.B765 1998
952.04 – dc21 98-38448 CIP

Third edition
ISBN 0 521 643732 hardback
ISBN 0 521 643759 paperback

For my father and my mother-in-law

What do I think the ideal image of Japan should be? Ours is a nation that prizes the best of its traditions and history, that treasures peace and liberal democracy, small government and international contributions.

Nakasone Yasuhiro, 1997

Your country was built on principles. Japan was built on an archipelago.

Ambassador Okazaki Hisahiko to an American
journalist, 1997

I have tried to avoid generalizations, particularly 'the Japanese'. 'The Japanese' are 120,000,000 people, ranging in age from 0 to 119, in geographical locations across 21 degrees of latitude and 23 of longitude, and in profession from emperor to urban guerrilla.

Alan Booth, *The Roads to Sata*

Contents

Contents

Preface to the first edition

Any attempt to capture the essence of post-war Japan in a short survey must appear foolhardy. The only justification for my presumption is that recent, introductory works on contemporary Japan have been surprisingly rare and understandably cautious. There are, of course, many valuable analyses of the Japanese economy (frequently laudatory), its defence and external posture (or the lack of), present cultural and social relations (changing but with propriety) and domestic politics (Byzantine), but few observers have been reckless enough to gamble all on a general history. Reputations may be at risk. Still the effort deserves to be made – if only to provoke others to construct their superior version of reality.

Should any reader feel tempted by this sketch to consult some of the works listed in the short English-language bibliography he/she will immediately recognize the extent of my debts and inadequacies. The derivative nature of *Japan Today* is a tribute to others' scholarship. Space alone prevents the naming of the many individuals whose works I have ransacked for information and ideas. The resulting pot-pourri is my responsibility, not theirs. I must, however, pay thanks here to Professor Hosoya Chihiro and my colleagues at The International University of Japan for their tolerance of an acerbic European voice in their midst. My wife Machiko also deserves more than a mention for her assistance with translations, and understanding over forays to Tokyo. Lastly I have to thank Ms Jean Jenvey for typing up the manuscript and Ms Elizabeth Wetton for her editorial work.

Niigata-ken
January 1984

Preface to the third edition

This remains an introductory survey of contemporary Japan. It traces the nation's story from Imperial Japan's belated surrender in August 1945 to the financial and administrative problems of March 1998. Since events of the 1990s have confounded my earlier optimism, much of this edition is a new text. Public figures who did not receive even passing mention a decade ago, now find themselves leading a less confident state against the backcloth of greater domestic and international scrutiny of Japan's current behaviour.

What was originally scribbled in long hand on the super-express that links the deepest snow country of rural Niigata with Tokyo, has been replaced by instant technology through the assistance of Mr Ben Hiddlestone and my sons, Luke and Henry. I am grateful for their wizardry and the kind editorial work of both Ms Marigold Acland and Dr Andrew Taylor at Cambridge. Lastly, I must thank my wife Machiko for her enormous help and understanding of all things Japanese.

Ogikubo,
March 1998

Abbreviations

ACJ	Allied Council for Japan
ANZUS pact	Australia–New Zealand–United States Security Treaty
ASEAN	Association of South East Asian Nations
DSP	Democratic Socialist Party
EC	European Community
FEC	Far Eastern Commission
GATT	General Agreement on Tariffs and Trade
GNP	Gross National Product
JCP	Japan Communist Party
JNR	Japan National Railways
JSP	Japan Socialist Party
LDP	Liberal Democratic Party
MITI	Ministry of International Trade and Industry
MOF	Ministry of Finance
NATO	North Atlantic Treaty Organization
NHK	Japan Broadcasting Corporation
NLC	New Liberal Club
OPEC	Organization of Petroleum Exporting Countries
SCAP	Supreme Commander for the Allied Powers
SDF	Self-Defence Forces

Note on Japanese names

Japanese names in the text follow Japanese convention with the family name placed before the given name.

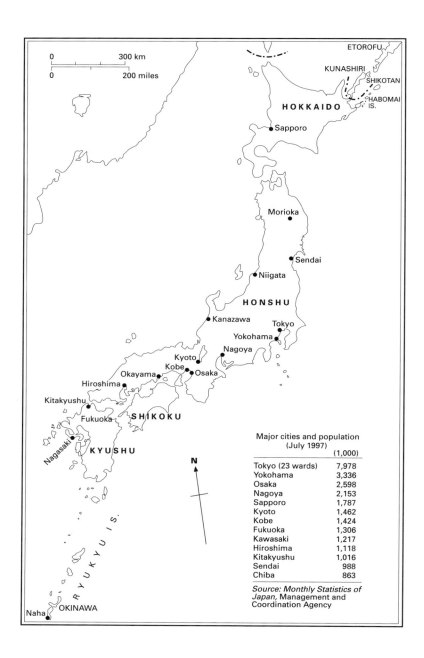

Major cities and population
(July 1997)

	(1,000)
Tokyo (23 wards)	7,978
Yokohama	3,336
Osaka	2,598
Nagoya	2,153
Sapporo	1,787
Kyoto	1,462
Kobe	1,424
Fukuoka	1,306
Kawasaki	1,217
Hiroshima	1,118
Kitakyushu	1,016
Sendai	988
Chiba	863

Source: *Monthly Statistics of Japan,* Management and Coordination Agency

Introduction

West London, late summer, 1997. On the darkened end of
the tube station at Earl's Court were two juxtaposed posters.
The first displayed an earlier generation of commuters
scrambling across a wooden bridge as the rain pelted against
their inadequate oiled umbrellas. The second assured
wilting Londoners and tourists alike that a lager beer
brewed in the traditional manner would best slake their
August thirsts. These displays on the District line were
intent on telling Europe the good news about Japan. The
arresting vermilion and green poster announced the
welcome arrival of a print collection by the ukiyoe master
Hiroshige at the Royal Academy in Piccadilly. The second
advertisement proclaimed the attractions of Kirin beer by
boasting that it had been bottled in Yokohama from the
nineteenth century and had the pedigree to win fresh
converts in the West. At the consumer level, Japan has
undoubtedly gained widespread recognition for its exporting
prowess: four-wheel drive cars from Nagoya, hand-held miniature video cameras and action comic books dominate their
respective markets.

From the neon advertisements in New York's Times Square
to similar signs on the waterfront buildings in Hong Kong,
the message is familiar. Japanese products are regarded

around the world as being well-made and competitively priced. Few dispute that Japan's industrialists have earned deserved praise in international markets and that nations as diverse as Britain and Thailand have benefited from considerable inward investment by multilateral companies with headquarters in Tokyo and Osaka. Japan is seen abroad to have won back parts of the reputation that it had seemingly lost for good through its barbarism in the Pacific war. The successes of the nation's industrialists and traders form the most widely recognized overseas image of contemporary Japan. It is the reputation of names such as Toyota, Sony and NEC that best symbolizes post-war Japan's reemergence as an international force.

Yet there is, of course, a great deal more to today's Japan than merely its impressive manufacturing sector and its huge general trading companies. Many Japanese, while undoubtedly proud of their nation's hard gained global economic and financial status, take as much or greater pleasure in the construction over the past half century of a society based on very different premises than those of pre-war and wartime Japan. It is the creation and consolidation of the values of a civil society that matter; the area that the present Emperor, in his first, and virtually only statement to the public following the death of his father, identified as the unequivocal maintenance of peace and democracy. No doubt such issues have been very largely taken for granted by the jaded youth of contemporary Japan and that yet more homilies on the necessity of maintaining the present, pacifist, constitution provoke little but boredom. I write, however, on the morning after one senior politician angrily denounced his critics, who have been calling for unanimous support for Prime Minister Hashimoto, by reminding one and all that the era of the Imperial Rule Assistance

Association that demanded absolute wartime conformity was over for good. Those abroad who imagine that contemporary Japan functions through a near total obedience to the rules of state and society might be surprised to hear former Chief Cabinet Secretary Kajiyama Seiroku tell his audience bluntly that Japan's economy risked going down the drain and that sound ethics rather than the present obsession with money ought to be the foundation of government.

Audiences overseas may also risk exaggerating the present economic difficulties that Japan undoubtedly faces and thereby discount the achievements of the last five decades. It is always tempting to write pieces that ask 'Whatever happened to Japan?' but it makes for better history to recall that similar uncharitable remarks have been made at frequent intervals since 1945 and that the nation has pulled through. Although, as this survey suggests, the 1990s have proved to be a miserable decade by the affluent standards associated with contemporary Japan, it would be absurd to start writing Japan off. Tokyo in March 1998 does not give the appearance of being the capital of a nation in permanent crisis, though the government has just shored up the financial base of twenty-one banks and insisted on the resignation of the governor of the Bank of Japan for failing to adequately supervise the conduct of his senior staff.

What is apparent, however, from Japan's current failings is the unmistakeable impact of the country's economic and financial troubles on the entire international system. The scale of Japan's overseas assets and the influence that this inevitably gives to Tokyo are a reflection of the nation's recently acquired strengths. The size of the Japanese economy guarantees that any substantial downturn must lead to jobs being lost in the City of London's financial houses, to fewer orders in the factories of the American heartland and to reduced business for the resort hotels and upmarket shops of Hawaii and Australia's Gold Coast.

The Japan factor is inescapable in today's global political economy. It is Japanese savings that help fund the American debt through the purchase by Japanese financial institutions of substantial quantities of US Treasury bonds, while Japanese inward investment until 1997 greatly aided the extraordinary advance of the southeast and northeast Asian 'tiger' economies. Since the World Bank predicts that it will be at least three years before such states can anticipate any effective recovery, the entire Asian-Pacific region must trust that Japan can avoid a substantial, deflationary recession that would further reduce hopes of an upturn in international trade.

For the present, however, Japan's mind is concentrated on domestic matters and public interest on regional issues is muted by deeper anxieties at home. The national mood can be judged by the holding of serious conferences with titles such as 'Japan's Last Chance for Renewal'. Japan in the late 1990s appears to have to confront a greater number of difficulties than at any time since the nation successfully completed its post-war reconstruction era and began to reestablish itself on the international stage. Yet younger Japanese, who have grown up with far higher material expectations than their parents' generation, have still to begin to appreciate the worsening prospects that they may face. The temptation in contemporary Japan is to assume that the state will be able to painlessly solve the pressing questions of economic and financial recovery, political and administrative reform and the new regional security environment following the gradual ending of the Cold War in Asia. The public still needs convincing that the institutions and practices associated with Japan's two generations of achievement deserve to be reformed or, in some instances, dismantled. The continuing strengths of the bureaucracy and the relative weakness of many political figures and business groups in the light of officialdom's general competence, make for difficulties in carrying out more than superficial reforms to the existing state structure. Perhaps it may take a deeper crisis before the rationale for change becomes unavoidable, though the necessary measures in such an emergency would presumably be highly unpalatable. Reform has become a mantra but not yet a policy programme.

We need now to trace how Japan began its journey back from the infinitely greater disasters of total war and Allied occupation that the nation faced in the autumn of 1945. What follows is a reminder of the obstacles that have been successfully overcome on the journey. It deserves to be recalled that virtually no one existing in the rubble of Tokyo half a century ago could have imagined that today's Japan would be able to enjoy the luxury of openly debating the consequences of such widespread affluence. It is all an improbable story.

1

Reconstruction: the occupation era

An army in uniform is not the only sort of army. Scientific technology and fighting spirit under a business suit will be our underground army. This Japanese-American war can be taken as the khaki losing to the business suits.

Tomizuka Kiyoshi to Okita Saburo, April 1945

The freedom and democracy of this post-war era were not things I had fought for and won; they were granted to me by powers beyond my own.

Kurosawa Akira *Something Like an Autobiography*

The Allied occupation of Japan was the consequence of Japan's defeat in the Pacific war. It proved to be a determined, complex attempt to alter Japanese institutions and behaviour through a combination of 'dictation and persuasion'. It took place under American leadership against a changing international situation which led ultimately to a pro-Western peace treaty for Japan. The occupation was dominated by the United States since it had spearheaded the crushing of Japan and had rightly demanded that its forces predominate in the garrisoning of the captured home islands. Japan appeared initially to be a demoralized and bankrupt state with immense domestic problems and the added burden of accommodating itself to the wishes of its new rulers. It was an unenviable position but one which Western public opinion felt to be entirely of Japan's own making. The Japanese people seemed destined to receive some of the medicine they had meted out to their Asian neighbours. There was much talk of harsh reparations, strict economic blockade and the ignominy of the arraignment of the Emperor for his share of responsibility for Japan's recent appalling record.

The occupation, in reality, evolved differently from the wishes of Japan's harshest critics. This transpired for at least three reasons. It was clearly difficult for the United States to employ Carthaginian measures on a subjugated people once its crusade to destroy the Axis military had succeeded. Governments can have consciences. It was also against Washington's strategic self-interest to leave Japan destitute and open to possible intervention by the Soviet Union. Lastly, the generally cooperative, if unenthusiastic, response of the Japanese establishment to Allied designs tended to ameliorate Japan's predicament.

The first few months after Japan's formal surrender on 2 September 1945 proved to be crucial to Japan's future. The principal allies, having concurred in the appointment of General Douglas MacArthur as Supreme Commander for the Allied Powers (SCAP), discovered all too late that he and his government intended to embark on a programme of comprehensive reform. It was a remarkable bid to change permanently the face of Japanese life and prevent a repetition of the circumstances which led to the militarism that had so scarred the 1930s and contributed to the Pacific war. For senior American participants, the early part of the occupation was an exhilarating dawn marked by challenge, confusion and not a little success. For most Japanese it was less an occasion to rejoice. The rigours of eking out an existence in blitzed cities and overcrowded villages left little surplus energy for celebrating the 'New Japan'. The Allies might be regarded in some quarters as liberators, but occupations, by definition, are almost invariably unpopular. It was more a question of accepting the inevitable in the expectation that this might speed up the process and lead to an early peace.

The choice of MacArthur as SCAP determined the character of much of the occupation's handiwork. MacArthur certainly received detailed orders from Washington but he contributed to the policy-making process by forwarding his own recommendations to the Army Department and the Joint Chiefs of Staff. While MacArthur was in general agreement with his nominal masters during the first three years of the period he had his own personal approach to Japanese questions. SCAP acknowledged that Japanese society might be capable of change if vigorous pressure were applied, but he was under no illusions as to the difficulties of making reform stick. He appreciated that Japan's long-term future would clearly be its own business – he wanted nothing to do with Allied supervisory bodies after a peace treaty had been signed – though he persisted in hoping that the occupation reforms might provide a firm foundation for a more democratic and liberal Japan.

MacArthur hoped, of course, that his proconsulate would not go unrecognized in the United States but Japan can consider itself fortunate in the choice of its occupation commander. MacArthur's approach to Japan was magnanimous in the main. SCAP intended to treat Japan in a manner which might lead to later more amicable US-Japan relations. He saw Tokyo as potentially of great value to his own nation.

MacArthur had few friends in the United States or among the other Allied powers for much of this generosity. It was hardly good domestic politics in late 1945 to insist on the retention of the Emperor, to obtain scarce food imports, to disown reparation recommendations and to consider an early resumption of foreign trade. MacArthur supported, however, the purge programme, particularly of Japanese army officers, and agreed with the establishment of the International Military Tribunal for the Far East to try suspected war criminals. He was also in favour of reducing the power of the Zaibatsu, the pre-war combines, and hoped that non-political trades unions might be encouraged to act as a countervailing power to these Japanese business groups. MacArthur's political sympathies were with the moderate left, despite his own Republican presidential aspirations, though the vagaries of occupation politics ultimately obliged him to deal for most of this period with Yoshida Shigeru, an elderly conservative politician who had a chequered pre-war diplomatic career.

The intellectual origins of the Allied occupation and the Japanese contribution to the outcome deserve mention at this point. SCAP GHQ was a military organization but some of its more influential officials were civilians. This created some tension between personnel who had held responsible administrative posts in New Deal agencies and the stauncher conservatives who tended to regard anti-Communism as an integral part of their mission in Japan. There were bitter debates between the reformist groups in General Whitney's Government Section and those eager to adopt a Cold War perspective in General Willoughby's G-2 (Intelligence) branch. Willoughby exchanged cigars for sherry with General Franco every Christmas. The more frequent victor in these ideological disputes was Whitney, though MacArthur himself could and did intervene on occasion to overrule his favoured staff. Allied and Japanese access to even the fringe of these policy meetings was difficult. The best prospect for unofficial representation was to build up a store of goodwill with MacArthur himself, or, failing that, with his senior aides. Use of more public forums such as the Allied Council for Japan (ACJ), which met regularly in Tokyo, or the Far Eastern Commission (FEC), which led a frustrating existence in Washington, rarely ended happily. MacArthur never liked to deal with either international body and made no secret of his antipathy towards what he interpreted as unwarranted interference. MacArthur's inner circle largely ran the show in the early years of the occupation. The British prime minister's personal representative to SCAP saw later that 'MacArthur *was* Japan' (his italics) and spoke of having been in attendance at 'the court of MacArthur'. Yoshida, who also met the supreme commander regularly, employed various tactics to gain an airing for his views. One technique was to leave behind unsigned memoranda after interviews with MacArthur. Yoshida, who regarded much of the reformist character of the occupation with the utmost suspicion, was not afraid to confront GHQ with his doubts. Indeed, it is difficult to think of any occupation legislation which had Yoshida's active blessing. He appreciated, however, that Allied land reform had saved the countryside from Communism, even though Yoshida was more interested after 1952 in demolishing sensitive parts of MacArthur's handiwork than consolidating or extending its ethos.

Yoshida's relations with MacArthur typified much of the Japanese official response to the occupation. It was, at times, less a question of the United States imposing its will on Japan than attempting to gain its cooperation in order to carry through its designs. Given the indirect nature of American rule (a vital and correct decision in the circumstances), there were frequent opportunities for Japanese bureaucrats and politicians at all levels of government either to inject a sense of urgency into a multitude of new programmes or quietly to stymie the process. The occupation was more often government by Japanese interpreter and official than American command; it could hardly be otherwise once the reform legislation became law. The further one went from Tokyo the more this became apparent. The pressing need to increase coal production might be recognized by all in SCAP GHQ and Yoshida's cabinet but miners in Hokkaido could hold a different view of Japan's plight. Similarly, local factors determined the extent to which well-intentioned labour reforms or taxation changes were actually put into practice. The occupation should not be seen as operating exclusively under a metropolitan dictat. Prefectural governors and village headmen often had the final say.

The United States' intentions in Japan were little short of revolutionary. It intended to reshape vast areas of Japanese life on the strength of its confidence in the blessings of American institutions, which had seemingly brought about Japan's recent total defeat and unconditional surrender. The United States' planners for post-war Japan believed that Japanese society was ripe for radical change (preferably on American lines) in its constitutional, industrial and social patterns. It was an absurdly ambitious programme, which sceptics at home and abroad thought doomed to failure. Secretary Stimson, drawing probably on his experiences as the senior American official in the Philippines, advised Truman in July 1945:

I would hope that our occupation of the Japanese islands would not involve the government of the country as a whole in any such manner as we are committed in Germany. I am afraid we would make a hash of it if we tried. The Japanese are an oriental people with an oriental mind and religion. Our occupation should be limited to that necessary to (a) impress the Japanese, and the orient as a whole, with the fact of Japanese defeat, (b) demilitarize the country, and (c) punish war criminals. including those responsible for the perfidy of Pearl Harbor.

British thinking, influenced by the reputation of the Japanologist Sir George Sansom, followed in very much the same cautious vein. But planners in Washington thought otherwise and gained presidential approval for a quite remarkable set of instructions. MacArthur was ordered by the United States Initial Post-Surrender Policy for Japan to make certain that Japan remained unable to pose a security threat to the United States and its Allies and that a 'peaceful' and 'responsible government' acting true to 'the principles of democratic self-government' was deemed desirable. To achieve these objectives 'the Japanese people shall be encouraged to develop a desire for individual liberties and respect for fundamental human rights, particularly the freedoms of religion, assembly, speech, and the press. They shall also be encouraged to form democratic and representative organisations.' Lastly, democratic political parties, with rights of assembly and public discussions were to be promoted and 'the judicial, legal, and police systems shall be reformed . . . to protect individual liberties and civil rights'.

There remained one important qualification. MacArthur was told that the new Japanese government 'should conform as closely as may be to principles of democratic self-government but it is not the responsibility of the Allied Powers to impose upon Japan any form of Government not supported by the freely expressed will of the people'. There was, therefore, from the first days of the occupation, a built-in contradiction in the approach to be followed towards Japan. It was far from clear how this tension would be resolved if, for example, the Japanese government, in its wisdom, were to resist the forced importation of Western democratic institutions and practices. Differences were soon apparent over a wide front.

The most convenient starting place for discussion of occupation reform is the 1947 constitution. It remains the foundation of the whole Allied edifice and yet continues to engender controversy. Much of the criticism later directed at the constitution can best be appreciated by examining the manner in which the document was written. The truth may be uncomfortable, but the post-war constitution was imposed upon Japan by the United States largely against the wishes of the Japanese government and its advisers. A small number of Japanese amendments were permitted by SCAP GHQ, but the constitution was an American formulation designed in the early months of 1946 to forestall the possibility that the FEC might present its own rival version. The constitution was less the child of the Cold War than the product of American unilateralism.

The Japanese and Allied gradualists who had felt that modification of the existing Meiji constitution might suffice were decisively beaten. The new document was concocted from disparate sources to provide a two chamber legislature with cabinet government on the British model. Supporters of the new constitution could claim that the process was a logical extension of 'Taisho Democracy'. It was maintained that precisely defined and greatly enhanced powers for both the executive and legislature (including an elaborate American committee structure), and the provision of female suffrage, an independent judiciary and a bill of rights were but the inevitable climax to democratic forces already existing within Japanese society.

This argument is not entirely persuasive. It tends to ignore the weaknesses of earlier attempts at parliamentary government and the mild repression of the war years. Left to itself the Japanese establishment would never have risked a constitution as radical as that imposed on Japan in 1946–7. Without arm-twisting and reminders of American military strength post-war Japanese politics would have taken a different road; conservative forces would have regrouped to swamp less reactionary elements even in the months following Japan's defeat. The new constitution was an alien import. It spoke of the individual's goals as 'life, liberty, and the pursuit of happiness' (article 13) and had to inform the Japanese public that the 'fundamental human rights by this Constitution guaranteed to the people of Japan are fruits of the age-old struggle of man to be free' (article 97). It was inevitably difficult to work up much enthusiasm for a document first drafted in English and drawn from a different political culture. Only gradually over the following decades did the constitution gain in popularity. It would, however, be dangerous to regard as conclusive the argument of its supporters that the constitution has proved itself since no amendments have yet been forthcoming. Such thinking ignores the immense difficulties of the amendment procedure. Constitutional amendments require a two-thirds vote of approval in each house of the Diet followed by a simple majority in a popular referendum. No cabinet would risk entering this area without being confident of victory. Attempts to alter the constitutional position of the Emperor or to revise the 'no-war' clause of article nine seem unlikely to succeed in the foreseeable future, although elements within the ruling Liberal Democratic Party remain eager for change.

Under the Meiji constitution the issue of where sovereignty lay had been unclear. In theory it resided with the Emperor, whose position has been variously described as ideologically absolutist and anti-modern. Such a view was promoted by the presentation of the 1889 constitution as a gift from the Emperor to his grateful subjects. Since the Emperor appointed the government he was the state. Later additions during the Meiji era left the political structure of Japan capable of being manipulated to extol the virtues of patriotism, filial piety and hierarchy. In reality sovereignty was located elsewhere. By the 1930s it was apparent that the military, assisted by political and bureaucratic forces, had won control of the Japanese state. It was in order to prevent any possible preemption in the future that the elaborate post-war constitution was propounded. Despite the hopes of some in SCAP GHQ it was likely that the forces of tradition would retain power after Japan's surrender in 1945. This had two effects. It made a radically different constitution essential to give encouragement to left-wing parties and trades unionists so that they would no longer be precluded from influencing their nation's future. Yet this involvement by Japan's left led also to exaggerated popular expectations of its ability to solve the country's problems, and contributed to rapid disillusionment with the non-conservative groups when given the unexpected opportunity to govern.

The failure of the Socialist-led coalition under Katayama Tetsu in 1947 was something of a foregone conclusion, since it had little prospect of containing – let alone solving – a difficult economic situation, yet it was under popular pressure to assume office and be seen to support democratic measures. It did little to enhance the electoral prospects for democratic socialism but much for the new constitution. It may have been political suicide but it was a necessary attempt to forge a responsible left-wing government. Kataya-ma's unsuccessful period in office proved to be the Socialists' only taste of power until the 1990s. The 1949 election returns confirmed the uphill problems which the left has had to confront since the occupation. It remained equally true until recently that, in the words of one disillusioned former Government Section official who had encouraged the Socialists, 'the prospects for a two-party system in Japan are poor simply because there is no group which can effectively oppose the formidable old guard conservatives'.

Consideration of the Emperor's position was vital to the progress of the occupation. It was also certain to generate controversy. Allied governments and the media had debated his future at length during the war and could be relied on to possess firm opinions as to his fate. At its crudest the issue was whether to arraign the Emperor for his nominal (or real) responsibility for Japan's expansionism or to employ him to further the aims of the Allies. It was decided by the United States government, with the eager support of MacArthur in Tokyo and the British Foreign Office in its representations to Washington, that the Emperor be retained. It was the only appropriate decision, unless the Allies were prepared to reckon with the consequences – possibly violent – of removing the head of the Japanese state in whose name the Imperial forces had fought and died.

By the time the new constitution was promulgated the Emperor's worth had been widely recognized by Allied diplomats, though this did not prevent influential voices from calling for his indictment at the Tokyo war-crimes trials. The Emperor was retained but he was largely stripped of his pre-war influence. He was no longer to be head of state, becoming instead merely the 'symbol of state'. His duties were ceremonial and precisely enumerated. MacArthur made the Emperor call on him and thereafter closely watched his activities. Thus, the Emperor's position in Japanese public life gradually changed. Today it is apparent that respect for his son's personage has greatly decreased among the post-war generations, although republicanism is not around the corner. The palace is required to perform a series of largely routine functions, which it undertakes with stiff dignity, before a variously respectful or indifferent populace. The Emperor and his successors seem likely to provide a sense of unity and continuity for some elements in Japanese society.

The two most important reforms after the new constitution had been drafted concerned agriculture and education. First land reform. This was instituted as much for political as economic ends. The highly ambitious aim was to create a new rural society where tenant farmers would be replaced by freeholders. MacArthur, pushing somewhat a false comparison between the United States of his youth and post-war Japan, intended that the sharecropper should be replaced by an independent yeomanry. The expectation was that the tenancy rows of the interwar years and the desperate poverty of large parts of the countryside might be avoided in the future by permitting all who so wished to purchase their own land. Absentee landlordism would be virtually outlawed and its political and economic influence destroyed for good. Strict limits were to be placed on the acreage allowed to any single farmer's household. SCAP intended to remove what he saw as the root cause of much pre-war bitterness and political extremism, since all too often a Tohoku peasant in the 1930s had discovered that life in the Imperial Army, despite its undoubted hardship, proved a less brutal calling than scratching an existence in northern Japan. The accretion of a little seniority made the discipline and regimentation of the army easier to bear. Junior officers were also thought to have been particularly sympathetic to the plight of their men's rural communities and eager to obtain a better deal for the countryside.

To be fair then to the Japanese establishment, there were pre-war precedents for parts of SCAP's land programme. But it would have been asking too much of this group to imagine that it would have voluntarily activated a scheme as radical as that ordered by SCAP. The occupation's land reforms (partly the handiwork of Australia and a rare example of harmony in the ACJ) meant that the pre-war landlords had to accept the virtual expropriation of their fields. Compensation was far from generous, but at least Japan was spared the bloodshed which was to mark similar reforms in China after 1949. Elimination of the Chinese gentry as a class was rarely accomplished in the Japanese manner of mixed farmer and landlord committees. The demise of the pre-war landlords left the way open for new political forces and personalities to make their appearance in the countryside.

The role of agriculture has evolved rapidly since the days when the demobbed Japanese soldier returned home to his village. The importance of agriculture as a major component of the Japanese economy has greatly diminished. The severity of the occupation's reforms left farmers with extremely small plots and the lure of new industrial jobs further depleted the stock of younger people prepared to put in the backbreaking work required to grow wet paddy rice. Today agriculture is in danger of becoming little more than a part-time job for the elderly. Farming is undertaken by many merely to gain the subsidies that leave some crops so highly protected that even partial liberalization would destroy the countryside and its political allies with it.

Political and economic reforms were easier to institute than attempts to alter the social structure of occupied Japan.

Many commentators thought this very concept of promoting a mass change of heart absurdly overambitious. As with other Allied schemes, the aim was to move fast before pre-war forces might re-assert themselves and to present alternative models and constituents that could fight off the temporarily discredited old ways. But Imperial Japan could not be instantly erased from history. Those who had been brought up in the Meiji period and returning soldiers who had expected to die for the Emperor were not easily convinced that democracy, equality and freedom were necessarily superior concepts. Besides, the poverty and uncertainty facing most Japanese after the war left limited opportunities for rethinking the past. Some occupation authorities recognized that it was hardly an auspicious time to call for a great experiment. SCAP persisted.

Evidence that the going would be hard was readily apparent. Public respect for the Emperor when he began his provincial inspection tours contrasted sharply with the lack of interest in the progress of the Tokyo war-crimes trials (the International Military Tribunal for the Far East). Memories were selective. With the Japanese family the inevitable centre of most people's lives at a time when individual resources were hopelessly inadequate, it was probably asking too much to expect more than lip service paid to new roles for mothers and daughters or any substantial encouragement to younger sons to fend for themselves. Individualism and personal mobility were the last things a hardpressed family needed to hear of. Women might get and use the vote, but their husbands frequently assumed that political equality ought not to impinge on masculine privileges. The content of education and the organization of the school system might change, but most of the old teachers remained. Values and beliefs could be altered only with difficulty.

19

Sceptical British observers foresaw that the results of educational reforms could hardly be gauged until the first generation of schoolchildren taught under the new scheme had reached maturity. Yet, as in other fields, such British and Commonwealth thinking was more than occasionally jaundiced. A start had to be made or the momentum would be lost. The reorganization of education was not without its problems, but it was a bold venture that permanently removed the ultra-nationalistic flavour of earlier Japanese schooling. Textbooks were rewritten, curricula revised, decentralization encouraged and the entire structure of education from primary school to university rejigged. The new system was to have its share of critics in the coming years, but it is doubtful if the ideological preferences of the Allies could have gained ground without such comprehensive reform. The United States, through the advice of its specialist Education Mission to Japan and the Civil Information and Education Staff section of SCAP GHQ, saw the conflict over the content and organization of education as the key to moulding a new Japan. It was one American 'hearts and minds' campaign that did pay off.

The Allies' motive for altering the pre-war industrial-financial combines (Zaibatsu) was clear cut. The economic strength of the four largest Zaibatsu (Mitsui, Mitsubishi, Sumitomo and Yasuda) was widely recognized to be unhealthy by those in SCAP GHQ wishing to promote economic democracy. The reputation of the Zaibatsu overseas and the belief that Japan's continental aggression was the result of an unholy alliance between big business and the military ensured that change was inevitable after 1945. The Zaibatsu had their fingers in too many pies to remain unscathed. A few select families dominated a few large combines, which in turn had a hammerlock on whole sectors of the Japanese economy. The system was controlled through the Zaibatsu banks. The big four employed financial obligations and personnel transfers to keep their subsidiaries and subcontractors in line. Half the financial business (banking, insurance and credit) and one-third of Japan's heavy industries were under Zaibatsu control in 1942. To the Manchester liberal and the Washington trustbuster this was all anathema.

Economic reform on the scale envisaged by some American officials would never have been introduced, but for the importance of the Zaibatsu to Japan's war effort and their close ties to senior bureaucrats and political circles. In 1947 seemingly tough antimonopoly and deconcentration legislation was approved by the Japanese Diet at the insistence of the United States. It appeared that there were to be structural changes to Japan's economy to deprive the old Zaibatsu families and groups of their former power. But the changes turned out to be considerably more modest than some had hoped. The family influence largely disappeared, but the shifts in American foreign policy towards east Asia following the evident collapse of Nationalist China and calls from the Congress to guard against unnecessary spending overseas left the core of Japanese finance and industry unimpaired. After 1949, Japanese reconstruction was more important than Allied retribution. The old combines regrouped and returned to something akin to their former status. Japan's post-war economic progress would have been severely hampered if SCAP's original curtailment programme had remained intact.

Valuable accounts of the contemporary Japanese economy have been written that exclude all reference to trades unions. To British readers, aware that union membership of their coal and railway industries once comprised 100 per cent of the labour force, this is difficult to comprehend. Yet Japanese industrial relations, for all their seeming differences and relative unimportance in Japanese society, deserve more than passing mention. Once again our starting point will be the occupation.

Initial American policies towards reviving and encouraging Japanese trades unions were in keeping with its aims of creating a new series of Japanese institutions which might counterbalance the old order. Unions had existed before the war, but their leaders had continually faced opposition from the police and industrialists. All this was to change with the arrival of experienced American labour activists and advisers. A host of legislative reforms, including the establishment of Japan's first Labour Ministry and pro-union laws, were introduced in the next two years. Unionization followed rapidly in most industries, although the benefits won by the workers were in constant danger of being wiped out by the hyperinflation of the period. The politicization of the new unions, which ultimately resulted in MacArthur banning a general strike hours before it was due to begin on 1 February 1947, was less to the liking of the United States. Changes in labour law, including restrictions on the activities of industrial civil servants who had been in the vanguard of strike calls, followed. Such acts – regressive in the view of the British and Australian governments – reduced the influence of important sections of the labour movement. Yet, despite these and later curtailments, the occupation's record deserves praise. Japan's labour unions, notwithstanding bitter feuding between rival left-wing groups and a strong tendency to organize on enterprise rather than industrial lines, had come of age by 1952.

Japan regained its independence with the ratification of the Treaty of San Francisco signed in 1952 after an occupation that had lasted from the summer of 1945 until April 1952. It was by any standards a remarkable period of cultural contrasts, changing policies and considerable accomplishment. The occupation era – yet to find its historian – is difficult to summarize. Much of the American literature tends to be written from entrenched positions, while Japanese commentators have been discouraged by the timidity of the Japanese government in releasing official documents and by the myriad conflicting memories that the occupation continues to arouse. To give a single sensational but typical example: one Japanese reconstruction of Yoshida's role during these years begins with GIs committing multiple rape, attacking senior Japanese bureaucrats and desecrating the flag. Television has a lot to answer for. With the Japanese public being reminded of the brutality and hunger of the occupation and the United States looking instead at its own generosity and idealism, it is not easy to envisage any future meeting of minds. Part of the occupation's legacy has been to leave very different national recollections of what the process was intended to do and how it was carried out. International understanding at this level remains a dream.

To return briefly to the international context of the occupation. Many critics of American policy in Japan held that the occupation ran out of steam long before 1952. General MacArthur had suggested as early as March 1947 that Japan had faithfully carried out its surrender obligations and the British government made similar representations to the State Department on numerous occasions. There would appear to be little doubt that it was American fears of Japan's economic and strategic vulnerability that delayed progress towards any Allied peace settlement. The onset of the Cold War and the strength of Communist forces in east and southeast Asia cautioned the American administration from letting Japan have a free hand. The eventual peace treaty had a quite definite quid pro quo attached to it. Japan was obliged to consent to the US-Japan Security Treaty on the same day that it signed the San Francisco documents. The left in Japan protested vehemently that this new military alliance had been dictated by Washington to perpetuate the occupation.

Under the terms of the peace treaty, Japan, at the behest largely of the United States, was granted peace that reflected the overall tone of the occupation. It was a generous settlement. Its critics felt it was unnecessarily forgiving and let Japan off too easily. Although Japanese sentiment did not view it quite so favourably – there was public dissatisfaction over the territorial clauses with respect to four small northern islands off Hokkaido (part of the Kurile chain) and the American retention of Okinawan bases – there was relief that the business was now over. The Japanese public, feeling that the occupation had been uncomfortably prolonged to fit their nation into the United States' Pacific security schemes, wanted only to get on with the job of rebuilding its economy. Reconstruction seemingly had no place for talk of rearmament and international responsibilities.

It was, however, impossible for the Japanese government to bury its head completely in the sand. A nation with Japan's recent record, its present human resources and future potential to regain its industrial position could hardly expect plain sailing. Like it or not, Japan reemerged after 1952 as a ward of the United States. But not even Washington could prevent the other Pacific powers from voicing considerable concern over where Japan might be going. Australia and New Zealand were only mollified by the creation of the Australia-New Zealand-United States Security Treaty (ANZUS pact), which gave guarantees that aggression in the Pacific would be resisted by the United States. Similar promises were contained in the US-Philippines defence agreement, while Manila and the rest of Asia that had known the Japanese heel were eager to gain all they could from later protracted reparation negotiations.

The San Francisco conference also had a number of empty chairs. Indonesia did not sign, though it made a separate accord later. India sat on the fence, since it wanted to lead what would shortly be termed the Third World and had no wish to antagonize its Himalayan neighbours. But a greater defect was the absence of any Chinese delegation. This was caused by the impossibility of an agreement between Britain and the United States on which of the two Chinese governments might be invited to the proceedings. It was an unsatisfactory face-saving compromise that was resolved shortly afterwards when Japan signed a treaty with Taiwan. The Soviet Union surprisingly attended but then predictably rejected the Anglo-American treaty terms.

One fear continually voiced by practically all participants and non-signatories alike was the danger of future Japanese expansionism. The United States government insisted that the rise of Nazism had demonstrated the impossibility of writing military restrictions into peace treaties. John Foster Dulles, the leader of the American team to San Francisco and the architect of the Japanese peace settlements, had attended the Versailles conference in 1919 and was frequently to recall the failures of the Allies' plans to contain post-war Germany. Ultimately, Dulles argued, the San Francisco powers could only trust Japan not to rearm in depth. It was an act of faith based on the twin assumptions that Japan had learnt its lesson and that the reconstruction of the Japanese economy and opportunities for international trade would more than compensate for its loss of empire. Events have so far proved

Dulles right. Japan's energies since the occupation have been channelled into developing an economic structure that is the envy of less successful nations. The tensions which currently exist with Japan's trading partners over its economic performance will be discussed later.

Japan in 1952 was once more an independent sovereign state. It could be reasonably certain that the United States would continue to assist financially and ensure the safety of the Japanese islands. Washington was simply unwilling to consider the possibility of letting Japan go its own way, since the strategic and industrial might of Japan (even the diminished Japan of 1952) was a vital factor in the United States' Pacific security system. To make this clear to friend and foe alike, the US-Japan Security Treaty permitted the deployment of American forces 'in and about Japan so as to deter armed attack upon Japan' and, if called upon by Tokyo, 'to put down large-scale internal riots and disturbances in Japan, caused through instigation or intervention by an outside power or powers'. American base areas appeared to many Japanese to have some of the unpleasant characteristics of the unequal treaties imposed on Japan in the mid-nineteenth century. It smacked of imperialism. Yet given Japan's own reluctance to rearm (Yoshida had prevaricated when Dulles pressed him to give a firm commitment) and the realities of east Asian international relations (the Korean war brought this home to sections of the Japanese public), there were few American alternatives. Hopes that Japan might gradually take over more of the responsibilities for its own defence were only partly realized later.

2

Conservatism: political continuity and challenges

The Japanese nation does not comprise only the working class. A responsible government must think in terms of the Japanese people as a whole.

Yoshida Shigeru, reflections on Japanese
politics, 1957

Schools and education facilities, rivers and dams, highways and roads, harbours and fishing ports, reservoirs and waterways, farm roads and farm infrastructure, streets, water supply and drainage works – the sweat of my brow lies behind all these projects in every city, village and town in my constituency.

Ohira Masayoshi, *Brush Strokes*

The conservatives still run Japan. Despite the plethora of new parties and platforms, novel electoral arrangements and politicians who have jumped ship, the Liberal Democratic Party found itself in September 1997 once again back in its familiar historical role as the majority party in the lower house of parliament. For all the sound and fury of the past five years, it is far from apparent that the political landscape has been irrevocably altered. What is clear, however, is that the recent developments have left earlier accounts of the political scene fit only for pulping. We must first review the gradual evolution of the political scene since the 1950s and then assess the shifts of the last decade against the remarkable stability of the first two post-war generations. Only then can a cautious estimate be made on the prospects for the future.

From 1955 to 1992 politics displayed few signs of the fragmentation and confusion of the present. Throughout the nearly four decades after the creation of the LDP in the mid-1950s, the conservatives held a remarkable monopoly on power. This contrasts sharply with both the coalition cabinets of the post-surrender years and the mid-1990s. The length of the LDP's hegemony was unprecedented. No other political party in a functioning democracy in the last half century has been able to boast such an extraordinarily extended period of one-party rule. The only European governments to experience control on anything like this scale were the Socialists in Sweden and the Christian Democratic parties in Italy and Germany.

The first years of the occupation were a period of enormous uncertainty. The intentions of the United States were liable to change and the volatility of the electorate further increased the difficulties of rival parties. There was much talk of how Japan must reform itself and aspire to uphold new democratic values. There was also a strong undercurrent of contradictory rhetoric that stressed the need to maintain Japanese values when facing a lengthy and unpopular occupation.

There were important continuities as well as sharp contrasts with the Japan that had fought in China from 1937 and then waged war on the Allied powers. In politics the campaign slogans might suggest a new order but pre-war politicians, bureaucrats, diplomats and labour leaders soon reappeared. All had to pay close attention to the hints and commands of SCAP GHQ, while demonstrating their ability to organize and mount campaigns for office. Some aspirants were simply purged by MacArthur's staff when their earlier records were examined, but the Japanese POW who had predicted to his Allied interrogator that 'unless you run the country from top to bottom for a generation, which is not exactly democratic either, you will have to take what co-operation you can find and not be too particular about it was surely correct. SCAP had to work with whoever emerged from the wash. It could only manipulate so far, if it wished to profess adherence to the ballot box. The consequences were decidedly messy.

The initial post-surrender cabinet was headed by the Emperor's cousin. After Higashikuni's departure there followed three years of political musical chairs. Governments came and went without much success in solving the economic problems which engulfed the nation. Although political parties changed names and leaders without turning a hair, there is little evidence to suggest anyone was equipped to take the unpopular decisions needed to salvage something from the wreck. Conservative cabinets by former diplomats – presumed to be able to ingratiate themselves with their American overlords – were as weak as the succeeding coalitions of the centre and moderate left. Only in the elections of January 1949 did the electorate give a clear indication of its preference. Yoshida Shigeru was returned to power with an absolute majority. The conservative hue of Japanese post-war politics was now firmly defined. Yoshida's Democratic Liberal Party swamped its rivals and ended the period of fluctuation and hesitancy. It would be relatively easy to argue that this was all on the cards and that the conservatism of the Japanese electorate was never in doubt, despite the 'reign of terror' instigated by SCAP. But it was not as simple as that. A more adventurous display by centralist groups and a less openly defiant stance by some labour unions might have made it harder going for Yoshida. He was, after all, far less popular in some Allied circles than he led himself to believe. His emergence as Japan's post-war leader – brought about initially by MacArthur's purge of his party boss – was, however, fully apparent following his 1949 electoral triumph.

Yoshida dominated Japanese politics during and after the occupation. His influence, through what became known as the 'Yoshida School', lived on long after his demise. Yoshida had an abrasive personality and was not frightened to speak out against what he saw as American errors in running the occupation. This earned him a degree of respect from General MacArthur and some popularity with the Japanese public. But with the conclusion of the peace treaty, his combativeness, while appreciated when Japan was prostrate, became increasingly distasteful. Yoshida, however, did not fade away. He clung to power, although challenged by rivals, including Hatoyama Ichiro, who had appeared certain to be premier in 1946 until purged by SCAP. Eventually in November 1954 Yoshida was obliged to resign. It was something of a fiasco at the end but Yoshida's reputation would later revive. If his last years were inglorious, his 'one man' legend appears secure. Yoshida was the first Japanese politician to make it to Madame Tussaud's and immortality in wax.

Yoshida's politics had appeal both for senior authorities in the occupation and for many confused and hungry Japanese who distrusted the siren calls of the left and the incessant rhetoric of people's liberation. First and foremost, the prime minister was strongly anti-communist. His daughter would tell the BBC much later on camera that for Yoshida Communism was like a red flag to a bull. He detested its alien ideology as thoroughly anti-Japanese but feared nevertheless that any drift to the left might lead to his nation totally embracing Marxism and all its works. Yoshida campaigned vigorously against the progressive political parties and their newly-empowered trades union allies. He saw no future for Japan under a state-controlled economy advocated by the left and was enraged by mass demonstrations that criticised his efforts to shore up the perilous industrial foundations required for any eventual national recovery. Yoshida pre-ferred to put his faith in the pre-war institutions of Imperial Japan. He strongly advocated the retention of the monarchy, arguing that to lose the throne was tantamount to aban-doning all sense of national identity and cultural cohesion. He was equally determined to deploy the talents of existing bureaucrats in devising programmes that might over time gain some remission from the hunger and malaise of the present. American officials and Japanese spokesmen alike were concerned that occupied Japan suffered from 'too many people, too little land and too few natural resources'. It is hardly surprising that the occupation era should be best characterized as the politics of food. Japan's economic plight was invariably serious and on occasion desperate. Insufficient rice, hyperinflation, rudimentary housing and uncertain employment all played into the hands of those critical of government. To make even limited progress under such conditions clearly took considerable talent. It is to Yoshida's credit that he was able to gain sufficient trust from MacArthur and his senior staff to keep Japan afloat.

Yoshida's departure was followed by major realignments in conservative ranks in order to ward off a reorganization of socialist forces. The challenge from the left spurred the Liberals (Yoshida's men) and Democrats (under Hatoyama) to unite in November 1955 as the Liberal Democratic Party

(LDP). Under this title the conservative coalition of disparate factions has held almost uninterrupted power as the party of big business, agriculture, the professions and small shop-keepers. It remains the case even today that the LDP 'knows only how to govern' and it is hard to imagine the party easily surrendering power to its more recent centralist rivals. The conservatives have indeed experienced fierce internicine warfare from the mid-1950s onwards but this has not pre-vented the LDP from remaining almost ever present on the stage. Despite an endless procession of scandals, factional knuckle fights and the eventual loss in the early 1990s of an entire section of the party, the LDP has usually been able to present at least the facade of unity and thereby win election after election. How this is achieved we shall see later.

In the 1950s political battles were fought largely over foreign policy. The left argued that the very peace treaty that had ended the Allied occupation was in itself a disguised form of continued American domination. The security ar-rangement, whereby Japan agreed to the stationing of large numbers of American forces throughout its archipelago, was widely interpreted as an unequal treaty which refuted Japan-ese government claims that Tokyo had regained its national sovereignty. It was all too easy for public opinion to draw historical parallels between General MacArthur's battalions and the 'black ships' of Commodore Perry that had forcibly opened Japan a century earlier. The indignities of Western imperialism in the 1850s appeared to have been reintro-duced in the 1950s. The occasional unguarded comment by American spokesmen that the United States was required not only to protect Japan from its potential enemies but also to protect the Asia-Pacific region from Japan tended to confirm the opposition's views on the validity of its com-plaints. The left campaigned vigorously for the immediate termination of the US-Japan security treaty that had been signed on precisely the same day as Yoshida had added his name to the peace treaty in San Francisco's Opera House. Incidents involving American military personnel and Japanese civilians have continued to the present to remain a source of major embarrassment to both governments.

Successive conservative cabinets attempted to walk a precarious path between American insistence that Japan begin to rearm in more than token style and a widespread popular revulsion against remilitarization. This pacifism was not the exclusive property of the Communists and Socialists. Many on the right shared these sentiments, albeit for somewhat less clearcut ideological motives. Business federations saw little advantage in diverting scarce resources to non-productive enterprises. Many industrialists took the pragmatic (and very Japanese) position that defeat in the Pacific war had led Japan up a blind alley. Japan's mistake was to lose. It could now best fulfil its destiny by regaining its economic strength and leaving the rarefied world of international relations to greater powers. Military might and formal empire were no longer a recipe for success; it was infinitely wiser now to concentrate on the less heroic but politically vital road of national reconstruction.

Popular agreement that Japan's first priority had to be the reestablishment of a firm economic structure played immediately into the hands of the LDP. The party of business claimed that it could be safely left with the task of restoring Japan's economy. The evidence was soon apparent. Already by 1954 the pre-war peak year of 1939 had been surpassed in the GNP tables. The years that followed quickly demonstrated the conservatives' skills at maximizing production and distributing, rather cautiously at least some of this new wealth. Double digit growth became the norm by the 1960s and the world's media responded in kind by beginning to talk of 'economic miracles'. The opposition had a poor hand to play against this newly gained prosperity. Its strongest suit was to decry rearmament.

The left was ever vigilant against what it interpreted as dangerous signs of nascent remilitarization. It deplored, as we have seen, the San Francisco peace settlements and sharply criticized the creation of the Defence Agency in 1954. The influence of the United States in the organization and matériel of the Japanese ground, maritime and air self-defence forces was an additional charge to be employed against the government. The US Army Area Handbook for Japan could note that 'the components of Japan's military establishment in 1960 resemble their counterparts in the United States Armed Forces in miniature'. (It was all a far cry from the days when French artillery advisers and Royal Navy officers had assisted at the birth of the Meiji armed forces in the 1870s and 1880s.) The left instead spoke of unarmed neutrality as a substitute for the LDP's pro-American defence and foreign policies. It set its sights on an end to the US-Japan Security Treaty, which was due to be renegotiated in 1960. The conservatives were well aware of the dangers they faced over defence. It was an unpopular issue with their own supporters, let alone the opposition groups. Public anxiety over Japan's limited freedom of action as an American ally during a period of intense East-West strain made it essential that the government be seen to gain a greater say in American strategic thinking for its Japanese bases. The result was to lead to Tokyo's most serious political crisis in the first two decades of the post-San Francisco era.

The ensuing turmoil overshadowed the earlier domestic achievements of Prime Minister Kishi Nobusuke and led to his resignation after he had forced the revised security pact through the Diet. Huge street demonstrations ended in violence, parliamentary tactics resulted in brawls, the US president's press secretary was roughed up, and a female student from Tokyo University was trampled to death. Kishi, who had the rug pulled from under him by rival LDP factions eager to profit from his downfall, was criticized from all sides. He had, however, won considerable concessions from the United States that made the security treaty less unequal.

The years following Kishi's departure were relatively calm. The political climate changed after the revised security arrangements had been digested. Kishi's successors, Ikeda Hayato and Sato Eisaku, were determined to emphasize Japan's continuing economic achievements and to play down any interest in the still controversial fields of defence and foreign policies. Both Ikeda and Sato (Kishi's brother, who was adopted into another family) wished to maintain close relations with the United States, while avoiding actions that might run the risk of provoking the opposition to remount the mass demonstrations that had obliged Kishi to cancel President Eisenhower's intended visit to Tokyo in June 1960. The jolt from this security crisis engendered a more cautious approach to alliance diplomacy by both sides from which the left could extract a degree of consolation. The continuation of what would prove to be decades of Japanese minimalism in the sensitive area of high politics reflected the anxieties of domestic opinion to regional entanglements. Foreign policy was widely seen as an obstacle to be avoided by politicians and electorate alike. There were no votes in it.

Not until the two Nixon 'shocks' in 1971 was the American connection reassessed by the conservatives. These twin surprises were spawned by the decision of President Nixon to alter the role of the dollar as the key currency in international trade and by his announcement that he intended to visit Beijing and reassess Sino-American relations after a generation of Cold War antagonism. Yet for all the critical editorials and parliamentary debate that these two measures aroused through the absence of prior consultation between Washington and Tokyo, it was to be economic dangers that belatedly brought home to the Japanese people their international vulnerability. The Arab-Israeli war of October 1973 was quickly seen as the end of an era. The high growth years suddenly became a thing of the past. The Japanese government under the leadership of Tanaka Kakuei, a horsedealer's son who had made a fortune in the construction industry, was beset by difficulties. The imposition of a severe oil embargo, stamped on Japan because it had followed the pro-Israeli policies of the American administration, caused an immediate national crisis. There was near panic. As the oil shock began to strangle the economy, industry was obliged to pass on its increased costs to consumers. Labour then retaliated by immediately pressing for substantial wage increases to cover its loss in real earnings. Inflation soared. The public beseiged supermarkets to carry away essential goods. The self-confidence of the state was dented as emergency energy-saving measures were rushed into effect. It was a critical period by any standards; the issue was more intractable than forcing Kishi to resign or putting pressure on the United States to consider the return of Okinawa. The basis of Japan's entire post-war prosperity appeared to be in the balance.

Yet the government held. For all the gross profiteering of business sectors and the hoarding by housewives, the conservatives were able to weather the storm. The Tanaka cabinet, largely through the efforts of the premier's rival, Fukuda Takeo, was able gradually to dampen down the inflationary fires, though inevitably at the cost of future double digit growth. Plans for greater pollution control, improvements to the dismal urban environment and Tanaka's particular interest in regional rather than metropolitan priorities were quietly shelved for the interim. Those economists who had been confidently predicting 8 to 10 per cent annual growth rates until the 1980s now looked decidedly optimistic. The oil crisis led to Japan reporting negative growth for 1974. Tanaka's own pet schemes for remodelling the Japanese archipelago had gained considerable popular attention prior to the crisis but were immediately derailed by the oil shock and land speculation. The prime minister, who had capitalized on a China boom by recognizing the Beijing government shortly after Nixon had visited the People's Republic of China, saw his popularity slump. In December 1974 Tanaka was obliged to resign over financial improprieties and was later arraigned on charges that were still before the courts when he died in December 1993.

Tanaka Kakuei's extraordinary political career would have been impossible to imagine in pre-war Japan. His rise and fall personifies many of the achievements and failures of the past half century. He will be long remembered in his snow-bound prefecture of Niigata as an outstanding native son who almost single-handedly lifted the remote region from rural obscurity into contemporary affluence. His political skills ensured that Niigata would be more than amply rewarded with lavish public works projects in return for continually re-electing both himself and his regional aides. Life-size statues to Tanaka can be found in Niigata as vivid testimony to his remarkable political abilities. He possessed the administrative and personal skills needed to gain an enormous portion of Japan's pork-barrel budget for the exclusive benefit of his constituents. The equally disgraceful side to this arrangement was the explicit understanding that each and every one of the construction and transportation companies that gained from these contracts were obliged to contribute a set percentage of all revenues to Tanaka's political war chest. The result was that for two decades and more the Tanaka faction of the LDP was a mighty instrument for winning and then maintaining a firm grip on power. Even after Tanaka was himself officially ostracized by his party, he was still able to determine who should be the next prime minister and what policies were to be followed by the incumbent. It was a decidedly poor advertisement for democracy and would lead eventually to the partial dismemberment of the conservatives and throw them temporarily into the political wilderness.

Tanaka was replaced as premier by Miki Takeo, a compromise candidate who had served thirty-seven years in the Diet before gaining the post. Yet Miki, for all his integrity, was only the leader of a small faction and dependent on the favour of others. His 'Mr Clean' image was exploited by the LDP. He was then unceremoniously dumped. Fukuda replaced Miki, only to find that his reward for improving Japan's economy was the loss of his job to Ohira Masayoshi. Ohira died in the midst of a general election campaign in 1980 – somewhat conveniently for the LDP it has to be said. His dissolution of the lower house of the Diet, when faced with intraparty difficulties and financial scandals, appeared to leave the LDP at risk. Opposition parties had expected to fare well in the June election but Ohira's death produced a landslide victory for the government. Confounding predictions of future coalition rule, the conservatives, this time under the loyal party stalwart Suzuki Zenko, ended up with an absolute majority. Suzuki, however, was rarely comfortable in his post and appeared to be relieved to resign in 1982. The LDP then elected Nakasone Yasuhiro to the premiership. It was a position to which the new leader had long aspired. From the outset he intended to use his office as a pulpit and direct rather than follow public opinion in a manner that many saw as un-Japanese. His attempts to gain popular understanding for a shift in Japan's foreign policies will be examined elsewhere. In domestic affairs he faced the constant embarrassment of being seen to rely on the support of Tanaka Kakuei and his political machine to maintain his position. The fact that the former prime minister was very much in the public eye over his continual legal battles to avoid the prospect of a lengthy prison sentence could do little to inspire public trust in the LDP and its leader. Nakasone was hardly helped in all this by the insistence of the Tanaka faction that the ex-premier should not be forced to resign his Diet seat while his able lawyers continued to fight on in the courts for their client.

Revenge was eventually extracted. In 1983 Tanaka received (and promptly appealed) the harsh verdict of four years in jail for misusing his position as prime minister by deciding the outcome of a fiercely competitive battle over civilian aircraft orders. Yet despite Tanaka's guilt in the Lockheed scandal – the tradition of foreign firms being caught up in Japanese bribery affairs has had a long and inglorious tradition throughout this century – the former prime minister continued to determine the selection of a succession of premiers and the appropriate policies they would be expected to follow. However humiliating it might be for politicians of the calibre of Mr Nakasone to be instructed over whom to appoint to the crucial posts of justice minister and construction supremo, there appeared to be few alternatives. All avenues to power were dependent on gaining the backing of the Tanaka School and its twin weapons of factional strength and financial resources. The process was continually deplored but rarely challenged in the 1980s.

Nakasone has proved to be the sole prime minister in the post-Tanaka era who would confidently stamp his imprint on events at home and abroad. Nakasone was very much the exception to the general rule that Japanese premiers are expected to run with the pack and wait until crises have emerged before attempting to offer compromise solutions. Indeed, Nakasone went out of his way to reverse this approach and quite deliberately courted public attention through frequent appearances in front of the media in order to distance himself from the conventional behind the scenes strategems of the political world. He was able thereby to demonstrate that Japanese government did not have to appear totally in hock to the advice of its permanent bureaucrats and the unimaginative demands of factional politics. Here, at last, was one Japanese politician able to refute Henry Kissinger's damning complaint that even after foreign nations had laboriously gained agreement from a Japanese prime minister there was rarely much prospect of that individual having the necessary clout to overturn the inevitable opposition that would arise once the consequences of change became apparent. Here, too, was a rare example of a Japanese politician who said what he thought and had something to say.

Nakasone was prime minister of Japan for over five years. He held power for longer than any of his immediate predecessors and his term as premier has proved to be easily in excess of those experienced by the eight individuals who have come and gone in rapid succession since he left office in November 1987. Only Yoshida Shigeru, Sato Eisaku and Nakasone among Japan's twenty-four post-war premiers have had the necessary skills to last longer than three and a half years in the post. Clearly Nakasone stands in contrast to the recent instances of weak prime ministers whose short periods in office have been beset with coalition and intra-party policy disputes. Yet to gain and then retain power for so long was never easy for Nakasone as his personality and ideas were seen by party elders as electoral liabilities. It was because of his aggressive character and the widely perceived nationalist stance that he had unashamedly expressed since first entering the Diet in 1947 that others of his generation were rewarded with high office before him. Many in the LDP would have liked to have excluded him from the premiership but eventually he gained his chance.

Nakasone relished power. He particularly enjoyed the opportunity to represent his nation overseas, claiming in the process a new position for Japan nearer to the centre of gravity of international relations. His successors have generally proved far less able either to project their own personalities on audiences abroad or to articulate with any clarity a position over where Japan stands on the pressing issues of the day. The manner in which the tall Nakasone almost literally pushed his way into the centre of the group photographs taken to commemorate the advanced nations' summits in the late 1980s provides a useful metaphor for what he was trying to accomplish for his country. Later premiers, with only a very few exceptions, have had less experience of international affairs and appear visibly uncomfortable when participating at global meetings. They have also had to face greater economic and financial hardships at home but, as in foreign affairs, the lack of confidence in expressing their own opinions is striking. Mr Hashimoto, for example, has been obliged to announce one economic revival package after another in which the contradictions between repeated promises not to increase government indebtedness and the necessity of yet more pump-priming are pronounced. Prime ministerial statements on Japan's present economic woes betray the thoughts and style of the senior bureaucrats who presumably scripted them.

This was not the Nakasone way of conducting government business. Nakasone's individualism was such that he always found it difficult to disguise his ambitions or to readily inspire the trust and support required to scramble to the top of Japan's greasy pole. Certainly this was a liability in the earlier phase of his career but once he had reached his goal he was able to turn this personality trait to his advantage. Nakasone came to power with the aim of altering portions of established policies under the somewhat grandiose slogan of supervising the end of the post-war era. He wanted to change what he saw as out of date practices and to create a more dynamic international role for a nation that he, as a former paymaster in the Imperial Japanese navy who had ended the war marooned in the occupied Dutch East Indies without a ship, regarded as unnecessarily deferential in foreign affairs. Recollections of Japan's defeat in the Pacific war and its enforced transformation during the American occupation and after formed the basis for Nakasone's political philosophy. He hoped to see Japan reevaluate the occupation reforms and to shift to a more active foreign policy that stressed active partnership rather than continuing silence and subservience to the United States. It was an ambitious agenda that reminded overseas commentators of somewhat similar programmes then being undertaken by Margaret Thatcher in Britain. Since Nakasone was only too well aware of the unpopularity of parts of his platform with entrenched political, bureaucratic and business interests, he deliberately took his campaign directly to the Japanese public by the use of television addresses.

Nakasone intended to educate both the Japanese people and their counterparts across the Pacific on the new realities facing his nation. The premier wanted to bestir Japan from its past timidity and to explain to the United States that an approximately equal partnership with Washington would necessarily require a change in American attitudes. From the outset Nakasone intended to create waves in a most un-Japanese fashion. Less than twelve months after gaining office, Nakasone was already being heralded as representing a new Japan that was prepared to identify with and speak up for the West. This was all very different from the behaviour of his predecessor, who had visited Washington in May 1981 only to become embroiled in controversy over whether or not Japan and the United States shared an 'alliance' and whether it had been agreed that Tokyo would defend the shipping routes of the South China Sea. Nakasone had long been portrayed in the Japanese media as a hawk intent on strengthening and revitalizing Japan's security forces, but he insisted that Japan had to make a greater contribution to the defence of its home islands and the surrounding waters both because of American dissatisfaction over what became popularly known as the 'free-rider' issue and, perhaps more importantly, because it was what Nakasone wanted for Japan. He had consistently maintained that Japan ought to take defence questions more seriously and needed to strengthen its own security if its claims to being a major power were to be fully recognized by other states. While publicly acknowledging that Japan's three non-nuclear 'principles' were to be respected, the new premier spoke of his intention to 'continue to build up a quality defence force at the minimum needed for the self-defence of Japan' and 'effectively maintain' the existing US-Japan security arrangements.

What changed in the Nakasone years in the realm of defence issues was not so much the pace of expansion (much had been promised at least earlier and partly realized) but consideration of where Japan stood and why it needed to proclaim its allegiance. Even the political debate over whether Japan should exceed the 1 per cent of GDP limit on defence spending can be seen as evidence to confirm Nakasone's opinion on the unrealistic nature of much earlier commentary. The figure had become a shibboleth devoid of any military rationale, though seen by the left as a guard against a retreat to the 1930s, and deserved to be scrapped. For Tokyo to move even fractionally over the previous defence limit and then for critics to proclaim that this was the beginning of the end for democratic government was patently absurd. Nakasone did succeed in asking more people to reconsider the basis for Japan's defence effort. In this exercise he was assisted by a gradual increase in public respect for the SDF's mission, which in turn was strongly influenced by a greater hostility towards the Soviet Union and concern that the United States was not the military force in the Asia-Pacific region that it had been before the fall of Saigon.

Nakasone's public endorsements of the strengths behind the US-Japan relationship were well received. By explaining that Japan had set its mind to greater cooperation in the defence field he was applauded by President Reagan and this led the prime minister in turn to boast of his personal ties to the president. The 'Ron-Yasu' tag gained Nakasone a great deal of valuable publicity at home and abroad. Nakasone's assertiveness overseas was appreciated within Japan as con-firmation that the post-war nation had come of age. The media attention, for example, on the annual advanced nations' summits and visits abroad by cabinet ministers was evidence of diminishing faith in neo-isolationism or editor-ials on 'Japan's position as a pacifist nation'. The claim of the

1985 white paper on defence (reported in the press on 8 August) that Japan's military played as important a role as Japan's diplomatic and economic functionaries in safeguarding the nation's security was taken to reflect Nakasone's own opinions, as was the statement in the foreword to the 1987 white paper which spoke of the public as having begun 'to take realistic views on defence issues in light of the real domestic and foreign conditions'. This was, however, only the beginning of what has remained a difficult case to put to the electorate. The director general of the Defence Agency still had to caution in 1987 that 'the people do not as yet have adequate interest and understanding concerning some matters: why Japan must make defence efforts and why Japan must firmly maintain the US-Japan security arrangements and endeavour to ensure and strengthen its reliability'. Both Nakasone and the US Congress were obliged to display more patience than they would have liked in the face of Japanese resistance to any rapid expansion on either the budgetary or mission fronts. The fact, however, that most new SDF weapon systems continued to be purchased from the United States or built under licence from American manufacturers undoubtedly helped to alleviate dissatisfaction in Washington. The 1980s saw regular annual increases in Japanese defence spending (and over foreign aid) which certainly led to the Reagan administration going out of its way to applaud this commitment, while still pressing Tokyo to do more.

Appreciation of Japan's new attention to security issues tempered US criticism of its Pacific ally's trading behaviour. President Reagan judged that Japan's new attention to defence improvements during the Nakasone years outweighed doubts on whether the country was acting unfairly in the economic field. To know and hear public endorsement of Japan's willingness to share in the defence of Western interests in the region was reckoned to be more important than penalizing Tokyo for refusing to import rice or silicon chips. The Cold War calculus worked in Japan's favour once again. Yet it has to be said that Nakasone's attempts to explain Japan's persistent trade imbalances convinced neither the American Congress nor his own people. Nakasone presided over an enormous expansion in Japan's balance of payments surplus and quite failed to persuade the Japanese public that it was ultimately in its own interests to begin to behave in a more 'international' manner. The prime minister's homely analogy that Japan had been for too long the mahjong victor who risked shortly driving away the other players from the table found few converts. Instead, Japanese industrialists and workers alike were no longer afraid to voice their belief that the rest of the world ought to stop complaining of Japan Inc. and its alleged non-tariff barriers to foreign imports and roll up its sleeves and fight back.

Trade issues between Japan and the United States persisted throughout the 1980s. The quadrupling of Japan's exports during the 1970s and a further doubling in the 1980s inevitably had a major impact on Tokyo's economic and political dealings with the rest of the industrialized world. All that can be said in Mr Nakasone's defence is that this burgeoning trade problem was an international issue before he came to power and that the prime minister did at least attempt to persuade the electorate of the potential consequence for Japanese society if the trade imbalances were not tackled with a sense of urgency. Yet Nakasone, in his turn, bequeathed to Mr Takeshita, his successor, an economy that was still almost too successful for the liking of Japan's diplomats. Newspapers and television bulletins in North America and western Europe continued to be filled with stories of record surpluses by Japan and threats of retaliation by US Congressmen and European parliaments in what were widely reported to be a series of trade wars.

No political party inside Japan was prepared collectively to take these warnings too seriously. For Nakasone it was the potential damage to US-Japan relations that caused him particular anxiety; he displayed far less interest in EC-Japan or ASEAN-Japan trade issues, since neither grouping had the security links to Tokyo that remained always of primary concern to the prime minister in his evaluation of global events. Nakasone's approach was to employ the dramatic gesture and rush off to breakfast meetings with US senators without really getting to grips with the fundamental problems that bedevilled the Pacific relationship in the 1980s. He would make frequent remarks on the need for new market opening initiatives and import drives but these ploys did little to reduce the trade gap. His much heralded promises rarely succeeded in placating the car manufacturers in Detroit or the timber exporters of the Pacific coast. Nakasone was no more persuasive with his own public. In the spring of 1985, at the exact moment when Japan became the largest creditor nation in the world and the US emerged as the country with the greatest deficit, his televised lectures elicited almost no response from Japanese audiences. The *Asahi Shimbun*'s poll on public reaction to the premier's remarks revealed that over 80 per cent of those questioned admitted that there were simply no foreign products that they wished to purchase at present. What the Japanese electorate expected from their leader was a continuation of his international charm offensive; this way they reckoned he could put his self-proclaimed links with the rest of the world to good use.

The truth, of course, was that not even as assertive a figure as Nakasone could begin to single-handedly shift the siege mentality of consumers and politicians alike. Post-war Japan had been told to save, cooperate and buy imported goods last. The establishment did not take kindly to Nakasone's efforts to alter the status quo and the fact that the premier had to enlist the support of his own research groups, academic contacts and ad hoc reform committees revealed the hurdles that he faced from the combined forces of bureaucrats and business circles.

Distinguished figures might consult with Nakasone in preparing reports on external economic problems but the political difficulties these blue riband groups frequently encountered when the time came to implement their findings mocked the premier. It was all very well for Nakasone to preach to the converted in his incessant campaign to internationalize Japan, yet the evergrowing trade surpluses demonstrated the relative feebleness of the prime minister in his bid to galvanize a hesitant state into action. He faced vocal attacks from both his own people and the wider world. In an attempt to confront his overseas critics Nakasone launched a swingeing assault on the structural faults of the Japanese economy. In 1986 he commended the Maekawa report as evidence of his determination to tackle what observers abroad were by now defining as 'the Japan problem'. The report, named after its author, who had previously been governor of the Bank of Japan, urged the nation to grow under its own steam rather than depend so heavily on exports to the United States and elsewhere. Evidence suggests that some progress on increasing domestic demand was achieved in the late 1980s but the temptation to rely on overseas markets when the Japanese economy came under strain at home remained ever present. Given this mind set it was hardly surprising that rival industrialists in the West would continue to campaign against unlimited Japanese penetration of their domestic markets. The seriousness of Japan's exporting prowess was seen in 1986 when Toyota announced that it had produced its fiftieth million car and then set the company's next target as the challenge to overtake General Motors. Competition with Detroit was seemingly unceasing, despite attempts by the US Congress to deter Japan's onslaught by the imposition of numerical limits on car imports from Nagoya. Beyond trade friction lay further trade friction.

Not even the very substantial appreciation of the Yen against the Dollar (endaka) by the late 1980s could do much to reduce the impact of Japanese competition. While some of its industries were damaged by currency changes, it would be false to assume there was any drastic 'hollowing out' of Japan's manufacturing base. Politicians were quick to pledge their support for all but the most inefficient sectors, realizing that public opinion was aghast at what it saw as having happened in the United States and western Europe when once proud industries were permitted to go to the wall. Simple electronics goods, cutlery and some textile mills were damaged but their owners then moved to virgin factories in Taiwan, Hong Kong and Singapore as the new 'tigers' of the Pacific rim modernized in much the same manner that Japan had done a generation earlier.

More important for Japan's future was Tokyo's rapid emergence as a dominant global financial power. If the trade surplus more than trebled during the Nakasone premiership, so did Japan's external assets. By 1988 the top seven banks in the world ranking and indeed eighteen of the first thirty were based in either Tokyo or Osaka. This rise had been more rapid than even the most optimistic Japanese government spokesman had expected and it appeared to mount a most serious challenge to the supremacy of New York, London and Frankfurt. Yet it was clearly in the interest of Western governments to encourage this massive inflow of capital, since Japanese financial institutions were vital to the funding of US Treasury bonds and major investors in such huge European schemes as the ambitious construction of the Anglo-French Eurotunnel project.

The world was now witnessing Japan's so-called 'second wave'. This phenomenon has its origins in the high savings rate of Japanese households and the inability of the nation's domestic institutions to absorb this tidal flood of money. Portions of Japan's savings from its extremely important post office accounts, banks, insurance companies and security firms simply had to be invested overseas if the Japanese housewife was to see even a modest return on her money. Graphic evidence of Japan's new overseas financial might was most apparent in the City of London, where over seventy Japanese security firms and nearly thirty banks had been established by 1990.

For the Japanese people, however, it was neither foreign affairs nor financial expansion overseas that was at the centre of their interest in Nakasone's long years in power. The area where Nakasone made his largest impact with the electorate was over the controversial issue of domestic reform. The prime minister adopted the theme of administrative reform as the hallmark of his government, much as earlier premiers had similarly tried to define their incumbencies with a single, pressing issue that required an urgent solution. Nakasone began by warning of the likely expansion in welfare costs as Japan reluctantly discovered that recent social improvements collided with an ageing society. The fear of an ever expanding national budgetary deficit was eventually sufficient for the Diet to agree to privatize former government monopolies (in the case of telephones and tobacco) and to hive off the extremely expensive public railway system (Japan National Railways) into regional entities. Yet there was fierce opposition to Nakasone's reforms and his bid to further extend his housekeeping measures into the vexed area of taxation proved to be a bridge too far even for the determined premier. Nakasone's drive to institute tax reform led to his downfall when the LDP felt it politic to continue pressing for special concessions to such loyal party supporters as farmers, doctors and small businessmen. Nakasone failed because many felt that his tax programme went against an electoral pledge that he had given before his sweeping July 1986 victory and others feared that the initial sales tax (set at 5 per cent) could be simply increased if and when a future cabinet judged fit.

Nakasone's years in power represent a rare example of attempts to speak with clarity and conviction in the often muffled world of contemporary Japanese politics. The difficulties that he faced, however, both in advocating substantial change to tame the state and in representing his nation overseas were hard to resolve when faced with domestic timidity. His bid to short-circuit the establishment and talk over the heads of the bureaucracy ultimately failed, since much of the electorate took the view that the problems of government were best reserved for those holding the existing levers of power. Against this conventional thinking, his own zeal and the judicious application of pressure from overseas governments were increasingly insufficient to win the day. His warnings that Japan badly needed to reckon with its administrative defects and act responsibly to avoid becoming once again 'an orphan in the world' were gradually disregarded. Yet Nakasone deserves praise for making Japanese politics more stimulating and for identifying many of the issues that still confront the nation a decade later. Nakasone's reputation is certain to be reassessed by future historians, particularly if Japan continues to stumble domestically and fails to exert itself more fully on the international stage.

Nakasone's long tenure ended when he personally selected Takeshita Noboru to be his successor in October 1987. The appointment was made by Nakasone in his capacity as president of the LDP, since all rival candidates were prepared to accept this unorthodox selection procedure in order to avoid the costs of a full-scale campaign. The new prime minister wished to distance himself from the style and policies of his predecessor by returning to the more consensual approach of the Ohira and Suzuki cabinets seen at the end of the 1970s and the beginning of the 1980s. The result was an immediate loss of sparkle in politics and a belief that the LDP should best avoid any ambitious programmes that might dent its newly improved parliamentary position. It was back to business as usual, though to Takeshita's credit he was eventually able to gain Diet approval for a tax reform measure that eliminated some of the more glaring inequalities in a system that had long left the white-collar workers out in the cold with few of the exemptions and privileges granted to special interest groups. It was this behind the scenes approach to gaining factional and even some opposition support that had the hallmarks of Takeshita's political manner. In public though he was always the grey prime minister, who spoke so elliptically that even Japanese audiences required translators to explain afterwards what he had been trying and deliberately failing to say.

Yet gradually Takeshita found himself embroiled in a major financial scandal and by the spring of 1989 his political future was under threat. As when tackling the question of introducing a more progressive taxation system, the prime minister preferred to avoid any clarity in his public statements. The result was that the details continued to dribble out piecemeal and the press smelt blood. The story centred on the activities of an ambitious information and publishing company named Recruit. It was to prove to be the largest of Japan's many post-war financial scandals, involving dozens of politicians, businessmen, bureaucrats, academics and journalists. Even nearly a decade after the scandal broke, the Tokyo High Court is still engaged in reviewing the cases against senior officials involved, who have been found guilty of accepting pre-flotation stock issued by Recruit's affiliated companies in return for favours. The former administrative vice-minister of education was given a lengthy sentence in January 1998 for having 'seriously tarnished the public trust in the duties performed by the Education Ministry'.

Takeshita was obliged to promise to introduce political reforms and to accept the resignation of senior members of his cabinet for their involvement in the Recruit affair. But the prime minister appears to have calculated that the damage could be contained and that his post was not itself in danger. The public suspected that Takeshita was being insincere and reckoned that his party was badly out of touch with the need to improve the glaring deficiencies in a system that permitted so many to benefit from substantial abuses of authority. The Recruit scandal finally led to Takeshita's enforced resignation in the summer of 1989.

Public dissatisfaction with the LDP was swiftly expressed in the 1989 upper house elections. It appeared that the ruling party was being punished for its arrogance in using its monopoly on power for its own personal ends, though some voters welcomed this opportunity also to signal their dissatisfaction with the tax reform bill. The national mood was such that even previously confirmed pro-conservative business leaders called on Takeshita to resign in order to accept responsibility for the LDP's ethical failings. There was now serious talk of a possible end to the party's reign as the permanent goverment of Japan.

While the LDP was attempting to defuse the Recruit scandal, the nation witnessed the long anticipated death and funeral of the Showa Emperor in January 1989. This did temporarily dislodge politics from the front page of the newspapers and its prominence on the television news broadcasts, but it cannot be said that the Emperor's death prompted any particularly profound debate on his sixty-two years on the throne. There was no attempt to encourage introspection on what his extraordinarily long period as Emperor might have meant for the state and people of Japan. Instead of trying to come to terms with the militaristic first two decades of the Showa era, what attention there was centred on his unprecedented cabinet intervention in August 1945 that made possible Imperial Japan's decision to surrender. While he was terminally ill with cancer (a fact generally known yet left vague in keeping with Japanese medical orthodoxy) portions of the nation went through at least the outward exercise of restraint out of respect for the Imperial family, but this was the end of the matter. It remains, however, very apparent that contemporary Japan is still deeply divided over how to view Tokyo's behaviour in Asia and the degree of responsibility it ought to accept over the Pacific war. Discussion of such subjects can still split families in the same way that it has polarized political opinion between those who recognize the faults of the past, those who insist instead that Japan was in fact the liberator rather than the enslaver of Asia and the silent majority who wish that the subject would simply go away.

Takeshita preferred to speak up for the rightists. He did his nation's reputation abroad considerable harm by adopting a characteristically limp stance over the war years. He noted that 'it should be judged by historians whether or not Japanese wartime acts were invasion' and only made things worse by his remark that it was 'hard' to label Hitler's moves in the second world war as aggression. In welcome contrast to these comments, Japan could take pride in the number of foreign dignitaries who flew to Tokyo for the funeral ceremonies, though many Japanese sensed that this was simply an endorsement of the economic achievements of the post-war era. Cynics reckoned that this 'funeral diplomacy' was in part an effort to maintain the supply of Japanese aid to the developing world. There was also unease over the constitutionality of the state's involvement in both this ceremony and the enthronement rites of the new Emperor in 1990. When a brave handful of Japanese Christian university presidents (including the head of my own institution) raised this question in public they were met with predictable intimidation from ultranationalists.

Politics, of course, could not go away during these months. Takeshita's resignation was followed by the LDP's search for yet another 'Mr Clean' who might yet be able to persuade at least portions of the public that the LDP was sincere about tackling corruption. In June 1989 Uno Sousuke was given the task of mucking out the stables without bringing the entire party to the point of self-destruction. But before he could do much beyond expressing his intentions, he too was obliged to resign. This was a consequence of the party's humiliation in the upper house elections caused by anger over his personal life and the unpopularity of the new sales tax. It was this fiasco that led first to Kaifu Toshiki and then the much more senior politician Miyazawa Kiichi having their uncomfortable turn as leader of a party that was in constant danger of dividing through its seeming inability to reform itself.

These proved to be the final days of uninterrupted one-party rule in post-war Japan. The LDP faced multiple crises in this confused period as it attempted to retain the rival factions within its always broad church, while reckoning with the collapse of the Cold War in the international sphere and the emergence of new conservative groups that wanted to establish an alternative to the familiar ways of running Japan. For some voters what mattered most were the extraordinary revelations concerning Kanemaru Shin, the old guard LDP boss who found it hard even to see the necessity of explaining why his residence was full of gold bullion and the proceeds of 'donations' from grateful corporations. Kanemaru was then the leader of the LDP's largest faction and his arrogance in disgrace was not forgotten or forgiven in the July 1993 general election that signalled the temporary demise of his party. Yet for others it was less the wholesale corruption that the Recruit and Tokyo Sagawa Kyubin scandals revealed to the nation and more the realization that the shifts in the global political system removed an important rationale for maintaining the LDP in power. Once Communism had collapsed in Europe, there was little need for a right-wing ideological defender of Japan's post-war status quo. It also followed that the Socialists too were in disarray as their party found it impossible to maintain unity in the light of the extraordinary changes in the international order. All this conspired to present opportunities for new, small parties that might be able to distance themselves from the two conventional groups in post-war Japanese politics.

The break up of the 1955 system was then realized at the July 1993 general election. It was preceded by the desertion from the conservatives of forty supporters of the ambitious and abrasive ex-LDP politician Ozawa Ichiro, who had long been complaining of the inability of the party to do more than merely go through the rhetoric of reform. Ozawa deliberately broke with the party, knowing full well of the consequences for both himself and the nation. As widely anticipated, the LDP and the Socialists lost support on a large scale and this led to the formation of an inexperienced and unstable coalition government under Hosokawa Morihiro, a renegade from the LDP who had made his reputation as the governor of Kumamoto prefecture. The ousting of the LDP was the product of very visible dissatisfaction with its recent performance and the ability of the small new parties to entice sufficient floating voters to gamble on the claims of these ex-conservative splinter groups. Once in office, however, the disenchantment with Hosokawa and his suc- cessor Hata Tsutomu was rapid, though it is probable that parts of the electorate were always sceptical about the ability of any political party to reform a parliamentary system that had long pandered to special interests and required massive funding to function at all. As if to confirm this thesis, Hosokawa was obliged to resign over financial improprieties after eighteen months as premier and Hata only survived for a couple of months before being ousted by the thoroughly opportunistic agreement of the LDP and Socialists to join forces in a grand coalition. The announcement that the new prime minister was to be Murayama Tomiichi of the SDPJ was greeted with disbelief in Tokyo; it appeared to go against the party's stubborn past and was felt simply to be a device to disguise the LDP's ultimate control of affairs. Former prime minister Takeshita said shortly after the deal with the Socialists was done that 'We have swallowed the Socialists and we have them in our stomach. All that remains is for the gastric juices to digest them.' It certainly looked to observers that the Socialists had been transformed into a pale shadow of their former selves, since they had already changed their name to Social Democrats and would shortly revise the entire basis of their foreign policy platform by agreeing to conform to the LDP's positive endorsement of the US-Japan security alliance and to recognize the constitutionality of Japan's own military establishment. Two generations of ideological opposition were promptly ripped up as the appeal of holding the premiership more than offset the party's history.

Murayama made a better showing as titular leader of Japan than his critics had initially predicted. He held office from June 1994 until January 1996, which in terms of length compared favourably with his immediate non-conservative predecessors, and he was able to make some significant alterations in how contemporary Japan sees itself and is, in turn, seen by others. His main accomplishments were to gain the final passage of a much contested electoral reform package that had begun under the Hosokawa government and to offer an apology for Japan's wartime actions to coincide with the fiftieth anniversary of Japan's surrender in August 1945. Both of these controversial measures deserve applause but Murayama was at times plainly not in control of events and seemed to need a great deal of prompting. His slow personal reaction to the devastating earthquake that hit the western port city of Kobe in 1995 was regarded as particularly unfortunate. The general ineffectiveness of regional and national authorities in the days after 6,400 lives were lost and parts of Kobe were destroyed led to much anger. Overseas observers asked why the offers of assistance of the United States forces in Japan and other trained emergency services from abroad were not accepted, while the sight of flattened expressways and buildings said little for the confident earlier assurances of officialdom that these had been specifically designed to withstand shocks of this magnitude. The country could only conclude that its cabinet and ministries had displayed major ineptitude; it was hard not to reckon that lives might have been saved if there had been prompter and more skilful coordinated action in the first crucial hours after the earthquake. Naturally the public wondered if other communities would fare any better should there be a future disaster of a similar magnitude in their locality. It is most unlikely that the coastal areas of the greater Tokyo conurbation, for example, would be able to resist the consequences of tidal waves that would almost certainly follow an earthquake in the Kanto region. Existing publicity on emergency procedures to be followed in Tokyo is sparse; perhaps with its huge population and the close proximity of residential and industrial zones there is little enough that can be done to prepare for any such eventuality.

Prime Minister Murayama also came under criticism in 1995 for the spate of terrorism in Japan linked to the religious cult titled Aum Shinrikyo. Here, though, the editorial writers had to admit that no open society can easily protect itself against fanatics who leave poisonous gas canisters on crowded metropolitan subway trains and the nation was far more interested in capturing the culprits than wondering if the police had been at fault in their tardiness to arrest Aum suspects over earlier violence. The eventual arrest and trial of Aum's leader, Asahara Shoko, left the Japanese public relieved that the bizarre cult had been broken up, but many asked how this 'supreme truth' new religion with its totalitarian indoctrination methods and merciless punishments could seemingly flourish among highly intelligent university graduates. No clear answer has emerged, though perhaps it was the creation of an organized alternative society that offered both a comprehensive ideology and an apparently secure bureaucratic structure that explains part of the appeal of Aum.

While the cult's ringleaders were being detained and prosecutions prepared, Mr Murayama resigned as prime minister. He had gained a degree of sympathetic respect from the public during his term in office, but he constantly faced difficulties, since the policies of his Socialist party had usually to be sacrificed to his conservative allies. In January 1996 Hashimoto Ryutaro, who had made his reputation in defending Japan's trading behaviour when sparring with Mickey Kantor of the Clinton administration, was appointed premier. The LDP was once again firmly ensconced in power with the first conservative leader of Japan since Miyazawa now heading the government. It remains to be seen if this presages a return to the policies and methods of the past or if some of the public's obvious dissatisfaction with the party will lead to a more open and accountable political system. The inauguration of the first Hashimoto coalition cabinet left Japan uncomfortably divided between the new and the old. The outcome is likely to be a series of cautious measures in favour of political reform without any drastic change in the fortunes of either the LDP or its traditional supporters. The party will probably succeed as long as the opposition groups continue to fragment and the conservatives prove they can run Japan's economy tolerably well.

3

Economism: growth and maturity

The first half of the Meiji Restoration motto 'strong army, rich country' was a dead letter, but the goal of 'rich country' at long last bore fruit in rapid economic growth.

Nakamura Takafusa, *The Postwar Japanese Economy*

I call the current situation 'a masochistic depression'.

Sakakibara Eisuke, 1997

The West is no longer looking to Japan with the admiration and anxiety of the past. Overseas journalists are now expected to report from Tokyo on the repeated sinkings of the once buoyant Japanese economy and the failings of associated business and political institutions. Sunset has all too frequently replaced sunrise in the newspaper headlines and sixty second pieces to camera for television. It is important, however, to keep some sense of proportion when noting the extreme contrasts between the rhapsodic tone of the 'bubble' years and the schadenfreude of the late 1990s. Japan, despite its recession-plagued contemporary form, is certain to remain a major economic force on international markets. Predictions, admittedly, on the twenty-first century emerging as the Japanese century are much less frequent than a decade ago but even a Japan attempting to cope with limited growth is still a formidable and indeed indispensable giant if global prosperity is to be achieved. The West today risks underestimating the sheer size and productive capacity of the Japanese economy; those who until recently rushed in only to praise the southeast Asian 'dragon' economies or the emergence of China do so at their peril. It would be foolhardy to neglect Japan. The nation remains the second largest economy in the world with a higher per capita income than the United States, low inflation and unemployment rates and a large and growing balance of payments surplus.

There is a distinct Japanese form of capitalism. The economic system in Japan is a mixture of free market competition and strong state intervention. One ministry defined this as a 'plan-orientated market economy', though entrepreneurs instantly reject such labels and point to the fierce in-fighting which undoubtedly does take place in some sectors. Yet the seemingly endless difficulties still facing the Japanese economy in the present decade have increased the role of government. Politicians and bureaucrats alike are constantly being lobbied to discover the magical elixir that might somehow get Japan moving again. Few would deny, however, that the role of the Japanese bureaucracy is one fundamental factor observable in any dissection of the economy. Its influence is substantial. Its prestige, political skills and policy-making power virtually allow senior civil servants to influence strongly national economic counsels. (We have referred earlier to the handicaps many ministers have to work under.) The Ministry of International Trade and Industry (MITI) has played an important part in encouraging the development of new industries, the consolidation of others and the cartelization of those judged to be terminal cases if left to market forces. Naturally it has had to face strong opposition to its recommendations from industrialists and rival bureaucracies, including the powerful Ministry of Finance and the now somewhat strengthened Fair Trade Commission.

What is noteworthy is not that MITI has made mistakes (its wish to reduce the number of Japanese car manufacturers is continually brought up to illustrate its fallibility), but that there have been relatively few major ones. It could not, of course, have its way on every occasion and its heyday was the 1950s when industry was more amenable to its suggestions. Yet even today MITI's influence is hard to avoid. New generation computer manufacturers and ailing aluminium smelting companies alike receive assistance from its officials. Key industries from the past usually get a decent burial from the ministry that sponsored their growth a generation earlier. Import restrictions, low-interest loans from government financial institutions, investment coordination and merger schemes are all part of MITI's repertoire. Japan has thus evolved a complicated series of state–private-industry relationships that work. They do not succeed all the time, but the results, at least until fairly recently, compared very favourably with those of any other mixed economy. New studies, however, have tended to belittle the efforts of MITI and suggest that it has been far less successful since the early 1980s. Its critics point out that recent advanced joint technology projects with electronics consortia have proved costly flops. But Japan's Industrial Policy – the phrase once enjoyed a degree of notoriety in the United States – would never have received its current attention if its bureaucrats had not first obtained the cooperation of industry, the financial community and labour. The best bureaucrats would have achieved little without the managerial and technical skills of Japanese enterprises. We shall turn to them next.

Japanese industry shares with Japan's Industrial Policy the brunt of foreign criticism of things Japanese. Criticism has expanded in direct proportion to Japan's increasing success. Understanding has advanced at a slower pace and has frequently been submerged under a barrage of harsh editorials, parliamentary questions and congressional testimony. Popular images in the West are disturbingly simplistic. Japanese factories apparently all commence with the entire workforce in identical grey fatigues chanting the company song and doing mass press-ups. This is followed by an intolerably long workday, punctuated only by intervals to attend Quality Control circles, with the workforce religiously spurning all offers of tea breaks.

Most foreign interest has been directed to the large Japanese manufacturing companies. These form the relatively small number of important exporters in steel, cars, machine tools, computers and electrical goods that have made consumers throughout the world aware of Japanese products. The high proportion of heavy and chemical industries in industrial production is clearly the consequence of government influence on Japanese investment patterns since the 1950s. Successor industries are, as we have seen, continually subject to some of the same planning procedures and scrutiny that launched Japan's post-war industrialization programme. It is to be expected that those that can demonstrate winning potential will again receive administrative assistance and that the less successful will be given little of what used to be the British-style 'lame duck' treatment. Losers are consigned to the scrap heap.

To identify the companies that make the news may now be in order. Japan's largest firms include two car manufacturers (Toyota and Nissan), Matsushita Electric, Hitachi, Nippon Steel (formed by the merger of Fuji and Yawata in March

1970) and Mitsubishi Heavy Industries. All are giant operations by world standards, though some have had to shed
thousands of workers in the last two decades to remain
competitive. All existed, often in very different circumstances, before the Pacific war. All are beholden to certain
banks for favourable opportunities to raise capital, and some
were part of Zaibatsu groupings before 1945. Employees in
such firms have a range of benefits unknown to less fortunate workers in smaller enterprises. The Western view of
Japanese industry is drawn from these major corporations,
with their supposed 'lifetime' employment practices, promotion largely dependent on seniority and company-based
unions. Large firms (defined as those employing more than
1,000 people) are in a strong position to hire the best
graduates and thereby perpetuate their dominance. Once
taken on, new recruits can expect lengthy periods of in-
company training and future attendance at refresher
courses. White-collar workers usually remain with their
company, or one of its subsidiaries, until retirement.

It is noteworthy that our list does not include any representatives from either the textile or shipbuilding industries.
Such companies were once world-beaters but, although still
important to the fate of many local communities, are now in
decline. Textiles had been the vanguard of Japan's pre-war
industrialization but by 1995 accounted for only 2 per cent
of total manufacturing output and now contributes little to
Japan's exports. Shipbuilding is following down the same
path as it encounters increased competition from countries
such as South Korea and Brazil.

Most of Japanese industry is neither large nor particularly
interested in exporting. Japan's dependency on international
trade is very low in comparison with most European and
Asian states. The only major exporting nation whose

experience parallels that of Japan's concentration on its large domestic markets is the United States; both share aproximately the same 8 per cent dependency ratio of exports to GDP. For Japan small enterprises concentrating on the domestic market form the backbone of the economy. They offer lower wages, far fewer fringe benefits and have less of the security associated with employment in blue-riband companies. The dualism of the Japanese economy, prevalent before the war, persists today. It was a product of a large surplus agrarian population (usually excluding the eldest sons, who were expected both to manage the family smallholding and look after their parents) that came to the cities looking for work. The result was depressed wages and low productivity levels. Since the exodus of the 1950s and early 1960s the wage differential has been reduced considerably but is unlikely to be ironed out, given the present economic climate. The sympathetic support given to agriculture and small businesses reflects widespread public sentiment that the nation ought to help certain endangered sectors of the economy through subsidies and trade protection.

In comparison with the United States, the western portions of Germany and Britain there can be little doubt that the structure of Japanese industry is quite different. Japan is, and will remain, the odd man out. It is a nation of small shopkeepers, family businesses and minuscule subcontractors. Workers on the Toyota assembly line receive a better deal than the sub-contracting panel beaters and turners who work for lower wages and risk getting the sack when times are hard. Nearly 60 per cent of the Japanese labour force in 1979 worked in establishments employing fewer than one hundred people. Only 13 per cent are employed now in firms with over 1,000 workers, which is half the American figure and only a third of the West German total.

The dual structure applies to the service sector as well. Japan, like other advanced countries, is already a post-industrial state. The phrase, for our purposes, means no more than that a majority of the workforce is engaged in the tertiary or service sector. In the case of Japan such a position was attained by 1970. In 1981, Bank of Japan statistics indicated that 55 per cent of all employees were then in service industries and by 1996 there were only 14.5 million workers out of a total labour force of over sixty-four million engaged in manufacturing according to Management and Coordination Agency data. We shall look later at the possible social implications of this gradual shift from agriculture to industry and finally to the tertiary stage, but we ought to be wary of those commentators who imagine this may prompt major cultural change. There is nothing particularly modern, for example, about Japan's immensely complicated distribution system. It is both a highly complex and strictly controlled mutual benefit society, which aims to protect a web of manufacturers, wholesalers and retailers. It does this admirably, at the expense of the consumer. Outsiders, both Japanese and foreign, are not welcome.

The situation is more promising in the technological areas of Japan's service sector. Yet it has to be borne in mind that almost 50 per cent of the thirty million workers in the tertiary sector are still employed in wholesale and retail businesses. (Japan rarely conforms to Western sociological patterns.) For those engaged in banking, trading companies (immensely important for handling Japan's imports and exports) and information services there would appear to be a brighter future. Technological research by Japan's 700,000 scientists and laboratory staff is designed to equip Japanese industry to face the future with a degree of confidence largely absent in western Europe. Japan does not win many

Nobel prizes and has no equivalent of the NASA Apollo programme or the Anglo-French Concorde project, but its introduction of computers and robots on a large scale suggests that it deploys its research for growth purposes. This is hardly surprising since private industry rather than the government usually has to foot the bill.

Interest in contemporary Japan has centred on its substantial economic achievements. The titles employed to account for Japan's progress – if progress it be – have made it apparent where many authors stand. Those in favour like to attach 'miracle', 'giant' or 'number one' to their books. Severer critics prefer instead to employ 'imperialism today', 'crisis' or 'ugly' as clues to their thinking. There is also a less adventurist third group that eschews all such frivolity and opts for strict neutrality, at least as far as the title page goes. Any questions we pose on the Japanese economy may, of course, reflect our personal prejudices. Still the subject must be tackled head-on. How did Japan make it? What were the costs? What might its future be over the next decade? What consequences could this have for its trading partners?

Japan was down but not out in September 1945. At first glance, however, the situation looked hopeless. The economy was clearly a shambles. The cities were frequently no more than rubble. The rice crop had failed. Repatriation of civilians and soldiers could only impose further strains on hungry families and confused bureaucrats. The Japanese empire had been liquidated. Countless Japanese had lost their homes and jobs. Yet the trams were running almost immediately. Shanty towns sprouted up overnight. Allied journalists saw how quickly the damage was being cleared away. Hunger led to rampant blackmarketeering and hoarding but the people scratched out a living under wretched urban conditions. (The farmers often did very well at the expense of the cities.) Any inventory of companies that today are international names will show how many were founded in the grim days after Japan's surrender. There were opportunities and some made the most of them. The nation – it never thought of itself as anything less even in the humiliation of defeat – had a host of assets which it could continue to draw on as it had during the war. Education, social cohesion and the spur of poverty go some way to explaining Japan's recovery.

The barest of statistics will tell one side of the story. The Pacific war left Japan without a quarter of its national wealth, since factories, offices and shops were gutted, the merchant marine had been sunk and transportation was badly damaged. Industrial output was slow to pick up and attempts to stimulate the economy merely resulted in hyper-inflation and low growth. Only by 1952 had industrial production recovered to 15 per cent above 1934–6 levels. The following year, as if to underline Japan's new sovereignty, was the first occasion when national income surpassed its pre-war peak.

The occupation forms the first of our five chronological divisions of the post-war Japanese economy. It was obviously an unpleasant period of food shortages, labour unrest and general uncertainty. Not until the 1970s was Japan to witness once again some of the tensions and confusions of an earlier era it thought it had permanently outgrown. Foreign verdicts on the progress of Japan by 1952 were decidedly mixed. John Foster Dulles termed the situation more or less hopeless, while the British textile industry was obsessed with what it saw as a Japanese revival that would kill off Lancashire. France and Australia also adopted a cautious approach to future Japanese trading prospects by joining Britain in resisting United States pleas that Japan be granted Most-Favoured-Nation treatment. All three countries blocked Japan's first application to join the General Agreement on Tariffs and Trade (GATT). Many Western industrial powers clearly saw the occupation as no more than a breathing space for their own economies. Japan, it was widely assumed, would quickly pick itself up. Its international competitors rarely doubted that a reconstructed Japan, aided by American financial assistance prompted by the Cold War in east Asia, would be back to renew its pre-war challenge. Events soon proved such jeremiads accurate.

The Allies' initial attitude to Japan's fate was simple and blunt. The victors said, in effect, that Japan had got itself into a mess and it was up to the Japanese to repair the damage at home and abroad. We noted earlier that, while such an approach lingered on in some quarters until the 1950s, it was quickly superseded in American official thinking. Japan was too important a prize to be put at risk. Revenge was forgotten. Reconstruction took its place. The Japanese government could only benefit from this rapid change of heart. It knew it was assured of American subsidies and food shipments and could (and did) pass the buck when economic mismanagement emerged. There was indeed much for the United States to criticize. Low productivity, high inflation, careless bookkeeping and a vast black economy were all part of the picture. Yet a gradual and patchy improvement did appear after 1948. This was an achievement in itself, given that the dislocations of the first post-surrender months had left GNP for 1946 as low as the 1917–18 level.

Management of the Japanese economy during the occupation retained many familiar features of the 1930s and the Pacific war era. Government direction was widespread throughout whole sectors. There was continuity of institution and policy – made all the easier by the infrequency of purges within the civil service. The national bureaucracy ended the occupation as firmly entrenched as ever. This was unfortunate but predictable when, for instance, ministers in the inexperienced Katayama cabinet had to have their hands held by their vice-ministers. Guidance to politicians and industrialists both before and after the occupation followed in the same groove.

The objectives of the first three years were only partially achieved. Getting people back to work and encouraging manufacturers to invest stoked up inflation and produced vigorous complaints and direct action from newly formed trades unions. SCAP by 1947 then began to reconsider its attitude towards labour and in 1948 the civil service unions were stripped of their right to strike. Efforts were also made to persuade the Japanese government to come to grips with its budgetary problems. If labour was disappointed with MacArthur's actions, the Japanese economic bureaucracy had to swallow its share of bitter medicine in 1949 when the so-called 'Dodge Line' was imposed on the economy. That it was required at all is an indictment of Japan's civil servants who had made the appropriate noises on price stabilization programmes but gave official preference to increasing national output. Under the Dodge programme – named after the Detroit banker who led the American survey mission at the personal request of President Truman – Japan was obliged to follow an austerity package that its bureaucrats had lacked the courage to recommend to their masters. Dodge's attacks on tax evasion, budget deficits and an inflation rate which was wiping out industry's debts suggest that much was amiss with the Japanese economy and its overseers.

Economic recovery was assisted by United States aid. The American journalist John Gunther was told in 1950 that 'the contemporary Japanese prayer is that God grant that

71

the United States should cease to be their overlord but continue to be their underwriter'. Millions of dollars of aid helped keep the economy afloat, since Japan's foreign currency earnings could hardly begin to pay for its essential imports of food and raw materials. When a unified foreign currency system eventually began in 1949, with a fixed exchange rate of 360 Yen to the dollar, many observers held that the Yen had been deliberately undervalued to assist Japanese exporters in their struggle to recapture Asian and African markets. The British, for one, were not amused. The outbreak of the Korean war in June 1950 was a godsend to the economy. The United States suddenly required the services of Japanese manufacturers and construction companies. Material for the Eighth Army and Fifth Air Force brought in valuable dollars. American 'special procurements' paid for half of Japan's imports in 1952. The Korean war-boom permitted the economy to take off at the same time as the country regained its independence. Fortune certainly had favoured Japan; the Japanese made the most of their good luck. Expansion continued. From 1953 onwards the managers of the Japanese economy were in unfamiliar territory, since the old benchmarks had been passed. The rest of the 1950s produced an unprecedented boom accompanied by a short recession in 1957–8. The high growth era was underway.

It is tempting to describe much of Japan's economic history from the mid-1950s to the mid-1980s as pre-ordained. Yet success was far from inevitable. The same popular ingredients were, of course, present throughout but there were always alternative bureaucratic options and paths not taken. Prime Minister Yoshida, for example, during the last months of his lengthy period in office threw out MITI's proposed schemes to develop Japan's heavy industrial potential. The schemes were, however, approved after his resignation. The twin objectives were to strengthen Japan's industrial structure, which in turn would generate exports and hopefully pay for the required raw materials, and to develop a larger domestic market for consumer goods. A nation that had subsisted on a military footing for a generation as either occupier or occupied was at last to gain some relaxation, but the relatively low priority given to personal consumption is testimony alike to government psychology and public patience.

Expansion both at home and overseas led to an annual economic growth rate in the late 1950s of approximately 8 per cent. This in its turn gave the Ikeda cabinet sufficient confidence to approve a much-heralded 'National Income Doubling Plan' in December 1960. Here was evidence, if the remaining doubters were prepared to take off their blinkers, that Japan meant business. The 1950s had provided the industrial foundations in steel, chemicals and shipbuilding on which later prosperity could be built. The Western image of Japan as the alarm clock and bicycle exporter was hopelessly out of date by 1960. Yet it persisted. De Gaulle is reputed to have said he was going to have a little chat with a Japanese transistor salesman. He meant rather an interview with the premier of the nation which in 1962 had a larger gross national product than France.

The 1960s showed growth acceleration that left even the record of the late 1950s in the shade. For manufacturing industries these were to be the sweet years. By the end of the decade Japan ranked number one in shipbuilding, radio and television production and was third in crude steel, pulp, cement, fertilizer and passenger-car output. Productivity increases permitted industrialists to plough back their profits in the shape of more modern equipment, which in its turn boosted production. During the early 1960s foreign journalists began to attach the epithet 'miracle' to stories filed from Tokyo. Gradually, some popular perceptions began to change. It would prove to be an all too brief period of Western applause before trade hostilities commenced.

If the media overseas were starting to take note of Japan, changes were also underway in Japan's external trade relations. Pressure began to mount from other industrialized nations to persuade Japan to liberalize its currency and open up its domestic markets. Behaviour that had been tolerated when the Japanese economy was under reconstruction could find relatively few defenders by 1960, and fewer still later when the pace of change continued to be slow. The Japanese government's approach to international criticism was to wait until the pressure became intense and then respond with the bare minimum likely to get the West temporarily to relent. Japan's propensity to import finished goods was low, and even in the 1990s has remained disappointing. Japanese tariffs until the 1970s were calculated to dissuade Japanese trading companies from importing foreign-manufactured goods that were currently available within Japan.

The government simultaneously built up nascent manufacturing industries behind high tariff walls. Many would contend that the Japanese car industry might never have attained its present global position without highly protectionist barriers in the 1950s and 1960s. It was often the case that the size of the rapidly expanding home market was sufficient to launch and then develop a product before attempts were made to crack overseas markets. Internationalization was seen by Japan's economic bureaucracy as something to be avoided until there were sufficiently competitive domestic industries able to fend off any likely foreign challenge. The evidence from a series of economic plans in the

1960s and early 1970s would suggest that neither the government nor the public at large had any quarrel with such nationalistic trade strategies. The 'promotion of international cooperation' was invariably the item consigned to the end of government economic and social planning reports. Due to the realities of the Cold War in the region it has to be said that Tokyo escaped rather lightly from American strictures on Japanese trading behaviour. The need to maintain close security ties with Japan undoubtedly led to a downplaying of criticism of economic issues until it was perhaps too late in the day.

Dynamic growth continued until 1973. Japan's foreign trade expanded at a formidable rate, unmatched by any other advanced nation. The arguments that some had applied to the fast growth of the 1950s were quickly shown to be out of date. The dislocations of war and the determination to recover did not lead to any reduction in economic performance once Japan had put itself back on its feet. Quite the reverse. Exports, which had totaled $4,100 million in 1960, reached $19,300 million in 1970 and by 1973 had increased to $36,900 million. For the period 1960–70 Japan's annual growth rate exceeded 10 per cent throughout the decade, aside from two short recessions in 1962 and 1965.

Even at the bottom of the business cycle the economy continued to experience a creditable growth rate. Manufacturing industries, aided by remarkably high reinvestment in new machinery, boomed. Where it had been unusual to find household appliances such as electric washing machines, refrigerators, cleaners and sewing machines in Japanese homes in the 1950s, it was rare indeed a generation later to enter houses without all of these consumer items. Demand for colour television and air conditioning also mushroomed with exporters again concentrating first on the domestic market and then preparing aggressive export drives at highly competitive prices. On the basis of such successes, economists began to pose very different questions from those of a decade earlier. Instead of asking when the Japanese boom would peter out, the issue became rather to estimate when Japan might conceivably surpass the United States. The talk was of the Japanese century and double digit economic growth through the 1980s and beyond.

It did not work out quite that way. International events beyond Japan's control quickly and unceremoniously aborted some of these wilder predictions. Simultaneously, economists began to refer to that suspiciously vague phrase, beloved of politicians, 'the quality of life'. It was (with hindsight) as if the ending of the supergrowth years had been replaced overnight by a new and seemingly more worthy human goal. Reference to 'domestic socio-economic structural change' and a Japanese 'welfare society' coincided with what the Japanese press termed the 'Oil Shock'. The economy, which was already in difficulties through Prime Minister Tanaka's ambitious yet inflationary political schemes, an undervalued yen and excess liquidity, temporarily slumped. It would soon recover, but the impact on Japan of the Arab oil embargo of the autumn of 1973 was profound. The public was being told that growth was not necessarily beneficial at the same time as it had to swallow an inflation rate in 1973 of 29 per cent. No wonder it was to look back nostalgically on the growth years, when the rest of the world was not breathing down Japan's neck and the social consequences of fast industrialization were not so readily appreciated. As Edwin Reischauer, the former American ambassador to Tokyo, aptly noted of the Oil Shock's impact on the Japanese: 'For them the world would never seem the same again.'

Yet new slogans rapidly replaced the old. The situational ethic which had assisted in digesting the traumas of defeat and occupation played its part in the public's accommodation of uncomfortable realities in the 1970s. If the quadrupling of oil prices achieved nothing else, it did provide a salutary reminder that Japan was no longer an island relatively free from foreign contacts. The aim now was to 'internationalize' Japan. The concept was decidedly leaky but it surely pointed out what ought to have been obvious earlier, yet had been continually played down by the government and the civil service. Japan, after its first Oil Shock, needed to win friends and influence states that it had previously regarded as little more than export markets or sources of cheap fuels and primary products. It had to begin to implement many of the existing paper commitments to liberalize its complicated import system and let other nations stake a claim to a share of the enticing but difficult Japanese domestic market. It had, in effect, to change its behaviour.

It is tempting, but more than a little unfair, to deride this switch as sheer opportunism masquerading as talk of new international orders and global interdependence. The Japanese government's policies were probably no better or no worse than those of other industrialized nations facing the threat of energy and resource shortages. Its responsibilities lay primarily with its citizens and their livelihood. To safeguard Japan's economic future it was obliged to reconsider its Middle Eastern diplomacy, talk publicly and work privately for trade and capital liberalization and convince Japan's business and bureaucratic elites that trade surpluses and non-tariff barriers might cause more problems than they attempted to solve. The period from the mid-1970s to the end of the decade might, therefore, be termed the era of reassessment. It was the occasion when Japan was obliged to review its post-war history and reevaluate its standing.

Japan came out of the 1970s in far better shape than either its economic bureaucrats or foreign friends could have dared to imagine in 1974. Two Oil Shocks had been overcome, most of its industries – the exceptions were sometimes important – had been opened up to overseas competition, and Japan had begun to make its first hesitant moves to export its capital to the West as well as to developing nations. Such measures were intended to emphasize Japan's new appreciation of its responsibilities to the contemporary international economy. The rest of the world took a more cautious view. It was still unprepared to share the optimism of the Japanese economist who could write in 1976 that 'the period of a disproportionate impact of Japan's economic growth on the world must now be assumed to belong to the past'.

Later events have left a host of international economic issues unresolved. Japan, in the meantime, had emerged once more as a nation with an impressive economic record. Growth was considerable by the standards of its main trading rivals. While western Europe and North America were still submerged in their worst depression since the 1930s, Japan had experienced an export-led recovery by 1983. The air, once again, was thick with charges of Japanese malpractices and immediate denials from MITI and the Ministry of Finance (MOF). The United States insisted that both formal and informal trade barriers prevented outsiders from being able to compete on a level playing field with Japan. The American media carried lurid cover stories on the theme of 'Trade Wars' and delighted to show Uncle Sam rolling up his sleeves to do battle with a gigantic sumo wrestler. It was apparent, however, that many of the less well-informed attacks on Japanese economic practices were no longer being taken as seriously as they might have been in the past. The Japanese economy was a different animal with greatly reduced tariffs from that of a decade earlier; the Plaza Agreement of 1985 also strengthened the Yen in the hope of bringing down the bilateral trade surplus. Tokyo had a stronger case by the 1980s and was becoming more skilful at presenting its arguments. In the end the United States and Japan did work out a succession of market opening measures in specific sectors such as farm products and telecommunications that helped dampen American criticisms but without Japan accepting the need to agree to numerical targets on its imports.

The contrast between the affluent and increasingly assertive Japan of the 1990s and the austerity of the occupation years is self-evident. Yet younger Japanese who have known nothing but prosperity find accounts of post-war deprivation of little interest. The Pacific war is recalled for the public every year with massive media attention on the anniversary of the atomic bombing of Hiroshima, but no group in Japanese society has any vested interest in recalling the indignities and hardship of the first decade after surrender. There is a large gap in the collective memory between the last days of the war and the beginnings of a more comfortable existence, which might be dated popularly somewhere between the marriage of the Crown Prince in 1959 and the Tokyo Olympics in 1964.

Certainly by the early 1960s Japan was on the way up again. Its recovery was over and the economy was now enjoying the benefits of what one Japanese economist and former foreign minister has termed 'the virtuous circle of accelerated growth'. Japan had made it; or so it appeared. But had it? Our subjective verdict will depend on the answers to two questions. The first is to ask whether the costs of economic development outweigh the benefits to Japan. The second will place the Japanese record within an international context and use European and North American standards, since Japan itself has long wished to be judged by such comparisons.

National reconstruction was the undoubted goal of Japan after the exhilarating initial successes and the later retreats of the Pacific war had ended in total capitulation. There were, of course, major differences between Japanese political groups as to how the economy ought to be organized and its fruits distributed, but few citizens needed to be reminded of Japan's predicament. Gaining sufficient funds to purchase food and fuel was most people's primary interest. Trades unions had much to complain about, but their leaders, in an admittedly difficult period, were generally a disappointment. The conservatives' election victory in 1949 was an indictment of the Katayama minority government and its labour supporters. Yoshida's new mandate, however, did not ensure any better economic future for Japan, since, even with his acceptance of the stabilization programme insisted upon by the United States, the outlook appeared grim. American diplomats were informed that Japan would have to put up with 'a deficit economy in precarious straits for years to come'. The Japanese smallholder, now working in his own minute fields, and the urban clerk in his rented wooden house, equipped with an earth closet and cold tap, knew this only too well.

Economic difficulties remained throughout the 1950s. The stress on capital investment was remarkable ('investment invites more investment' was the slogan of the 1961 white paper from the Economic Planning Agency), though the generation to gain most from such endeavours was the children of parents who put in the long hours in factories and offices after the war. There was a lengthy and quite deliberate time-lag before the Japanese government and its officials gave serious thought to much beyond higher wages. As the Anglo-Japanese novelist Ishiguro Kazuo was to write later of the occupants of a new jerry-built apartment block in Nagasaki during the 1950s, 'we were all of us waiting for the day we could move to something better'.

Critics of Yoshida complained that 'everything was economy, everything was efficiency'. Yet the election returns for the next two decades make it apparent that this had broad popular appeal. The left might warn of remilitarization and subordinate independence under the American anti-Communist banner in Asia, but the conservatives moved slowly over defence and took pains to minimize budgetary allocations to the Self-Defence Forces. The Income-Doubling Plan of 1960 was highly popular and 'wildly overfulfilled'. It was now the turn of the 'three Cs' (car, cooler and colour TV) to replace the 'three Sacred Treasures' (washing machine, refrigerator and black and white TV). Unemployment was minimal, wages and savings ratios were up and the Japanese Housing Corporation's first apartment complexes were being rented to those fortunate enough to qualify. The opening of the Shinkansen bullet train service between Tokyo and Osaka in October 1964, to coincide with the Tokyo Olympics, was further confirmation of Japanese engineering prowess and the occasion for not a little self-congratulation. The fastest train network in the world, the gaining of membership of the OECD and an economy shortly to overtake West Germany's suggested, as one Japanese novelist wrote of the opening ceremonies of the Olympics, that 'Japan had finally regained its national competency'.

The last major Japanese prestige event before a greater awareness of the strains of industrialization emerged was EXPO '70. It is a convenient symbol of where Japan stood on the eve of global currency and fuel crises. The crowds at the international exhibition site near Osaka were vast, patient and uncritical. It was a mass celebration of an urban future that was swamped by too many people in too small a space. The carnival for Japan was soon to be temporarily over. The 1970s were to be harder years.

It was time to take stock. The Japanese people had worked their passage back from poverty to a formidable ranking in the international economic pecking order. Yet, obviously, the size of the economy was no more than one yardstick by which to determine the state of the nation. Critics could suggest that incidences of poverty, income distribution statistics, per capita wealth housing conditions, the extent of social mobility and size of welfare payments presented a less rosy picture. There was a degree of truth in all these complaints. The government had ignored social infrastructure in order that industry should receive first priority. Metropolitan housing and recreational facilities were inadequate. Pensions were small. Still, popular perceptions were not greatly changed by press opposition to what has been termed 'social deprivation'. Public opinion polls have shown that the bulk of the Japanese people have since the late 1960s seen themselves as middle-class. Overseas commentators were often struck more by the lack of urban initiative to demand improvement in the face of environmental and housing deficiencies than the vigour of protest movements. Acquiescence was the usual response. Improved salaries left most Japanese unmoved by the thought of collective action. The economy might have its shortcomings but few wished personally to confront these consequences.

The left's theoreticians had reason enough to castigate the Japanese government for playing down the social costs of economic growth until the 1970s. There were serious gaps in some areas of what, rather late in the day, aspired to be a 'welfare society'. Much has since altered for the better. Yet these improvements have been not infrequently overlooked in the West. European opinion maintains, to quote *The Economist*'s special survey on Japan in July 1983, that 'Japan's infrastructure is little better than a developing country's'. The reality is less damning and even the recent disappointing rates of economic growth have not prevented substantial gains, particularly in the construction of new facilities such as schools and recreational centres that both benefit the community and provide employment and substantial profits for Japan's huge and politically influential construction industry. Private housing, however, continues to be excessively expensive, despite falls in urban residential land prices in the 1990s. National Land Agency statistics for January 1994 report that the average cost of a single house in Tokyo was a staggering 12.9 times annual income, in comparison with multiples of 6.9 for London and 2.9 for New York, while the average house price in Tokyo was then selling at four times the cost of comparable housing in New York.

'Quality of life' is a suggestive phrase but one perhaps capable of only approximate definition. Its advocates at times offer it as a synonym for the welfare state or as a stick with which to beat free-market economists. For our purposes it will be employed to reflect changing social and political values, which lay less stress on production per se as Japan hesitantly ponders the consequences of its rapid industrialization. Two cautions must immediately be noted. Economic growth is still the popular aspiration and the doubts implied in 'quality of life' criticisms are not widespread. Japan's own breed of capitalism is not under siege. (Historians, as 'Mr Dooley' said of the American Supreme Court, are obliged to follow the election returns.) Secondly, if social welfare is inadequate in some areas, there are other indicators that show Japan in a favourable light by even the most rigorous international comparison.

Health and education are two important social welfare provisions in which Japan has been up with the front-runners. Life expectancy for the Japanese is among the very highest in the world. For females the average Japanese life expectancy at birth is 82.3 years. For males it is 76.4 years, according to OECD data published in Paris in 1997. We shall look later at the demographic changes in store for Japan over the next two generations and the effects this will probably have on Japanese society in general. For the moment we can assume that improved post-war medical care and dietary changes have contributed to a nation that is now living thirty-five years longer than its citizens born at the end of the Taisho period (1926). Japan's provision of hospital beds per thousand people was the highest in the world in 1970, though its number of doctors was lower than its hospital record might suggest. Still, hospital care is good, particularly at the infant level. (Older doctors continue to keep their medical records in German.)

Improvements in education can be welcomed, though here again qualification will be necessary later. The change in length of education received by differing age groups within Japanese society is instructive and a source of considerable pride. In 1980, 37.9 per cent of the relevant age group were attending some form of tertiary education. The mass diploma society had arrived. While further diffusion of higher education will probably grow more slowly in the future, the percentage of youths continuing on to senior high school (at the age of fifteen) is over 95 per cent. This level was far in excess of the situation that existed until recent education reforms in some English-speaking countries.

Japan has also a first-class inter-city train network. After the Tokyo-Osaka line was completed, the Shinkansen spread south to Kyushu, and later in 1983, north and westward as LDP politicians demanded yet more lines and stations to satisfy their constituents, almost without regard to cost. Tanaka Kakuei even took the highly convenient (for my colleagues and the inhabitants of a few isolated hamlets) but absurd step of ordering the Joetsu Shinkansen to stop at a remote location near to the International University of Japan in Niigata prefecture, where the length of the specially constructed station platforms exceeds the geographical boundaries of the village. The more rural regions are clearly benefiting from their improved communications with the Tokyo-Nagoya-Osaka industrial centres. The service is fast, punctual and safe. In addition, national highways (totalling over 5,000 km by 1992 and with plans in hand to double this in the next decade) have been constructed, often to run in the same narrow coastal belt parallel to the Shinkansen. Passengers and goods can be transported at high speed from one urban centre to the next, but neither commuters nor freight-liners can avoid the inner urban congestion. The roads into the city centres on weekdays (Monday to Saturday still for some Japanese) are rarely less than crowded, while the situation on commuter trains from the suburbs to business districts is indeed an endurance test. Commuting depends equally on the efficiency of the train system and the tolerance of its passengers. The service is fast, punctual and unpleasant.

Writing in 1958, Kenneth Galbraith began the first page of his work *The Affluent Society* by defining the nations of wealth as those 'in the comparatively small corner of the world populated by Europeans'. Neither there nor anywhere else in his book did Japan receive any recognition. It was to be slightly different fifteen years later when he published

Economics and the Public Purpose, and today it is obviously impossible to ignore Japan in any extended discussion of contemporary economic development. European and North American interest in Japan's present economic position – a combination of admiration and secret longing that Japan might slip up on its own banana skin – has greatly increased since the days of *The Affluent Society* and will, we may safely assume, continue to do so.

Galbraith (who was involved in the United States Strategic Bombing Survey of Germany and Japan at the end of the war) might, however, be a convenient source of some strictures against the Japan of the first three post-war decades. The god of production had few rivals and certainly no equal. Higher growth was a national obsession and is still an essential goal. The attention given to a continuing spate of governmental and private economic forecasts by the press confirms this. There was, and there undoubtedly remains, considerable wariness against public expenditure. Much of Galbraith's anger at the United States of the Edsel Era (Ford's ill-fated model was launched in the same week as the Soviet Union put the Sputnik into space) could be applied to the Japan of the high growth era. Civic amenities were played down, roads were built without much thought as to whether a slow-moving stream of cars into Tokyo did anything but pollute an already noxious atmosphere and manufacturers refused to imagine there might be a finite number to the electrical goods that the Japanese household could be persuaded to purchase. The market has clearly not achieved all that the Keidanren would have us believe. The result is the lop-sided Japan of today.

Since then, however, the worst pollution problems have been overcome. Japan's present fuel exhaust regulations are stricter than Britain's. Photo-chemical smog has disappeared.

(The idea that Tokyo's traffic policemen are obliged to wear oxygen masks to survive is another firmly entrenched foreign myth.) At last the sewage system is also being improved and the habit of connecting effluent and storm drains is on the way out. It is not going to make headlines or win a single vote, but one of Japan's more laudable goals is to attain European levels of sewage disposal by the year 2000. Equally sensible are plans gradually to enlarge the park and recreational levels in Japan's metropolitan wastelands. 'Green Associations' are in their infancy (modelled on Britain's National Trust), yet they too demonstrate a belated attempt to prevent the total denuding of what remains of the natural environment on the outskirts of the urban complexes. Public attitudes may be slowly changing and politicians at both the national and local level appear to be readier to listen. It can at least be said that the rhetoric has altered. Prime Minister Nakasone was the first to refer to 'environmental beautification' and to start what is now a well established theme of parliamentary policy statements.

Substantial improvement has since been underway in a variety of fields, which may collectively be described as contributing to the betterment of Japan's 'quality of life'. Health, education, the urban environment and housing are widely accepted criteria that help determine what article twenty-five of the constitution calls 'the promotion and extension of social welfare and security'. The advances made possible here by economic growth have been very considerable. Gaps, it is certainly true, remain, but it seems reasonable to assume that a gradual improvement in such areas as metropolitan housing may be possible. Appearances, too, can be slightly misleading. Visitors arriving armed with phrases such as 'rabbit hutches' may be in danger of prejudging Japan's largest city .

Tokyo is admittedly an urban planner's nightmare. The capital's unprepossessing appearance is legendary. Yet this facade disguises a different reality of a metropolis with immense strengths and resilience. Grandparents who can recall the Kanto earthquake of 1923, the fire-bombings that devastated whole sections of the city in 1945 and the early post-war austerity have reason to boast. Ignore the skyscrapers of the central business districts – awash with blue suits during the day – and downtown Tokyo is a patchwork of bath houses, pachinko parlours, game centres, stand bars and tenements, in competition with factories, timberyards, offices and school playgrounds for the precious space. Motorways (constructed for the 1964 Tokyo Olympics) weave overhead to add to the noise and neon. It is rarely pretty, but Tokyo is undeniably alive in contrast to some European and American inner cities.

Only slightly less higgledy-piggledy lie the suburbs. Here bicycle lots threaten to engulf the train stations and two-storey tiled houses, fish shops, company dormitories and yet more bars offer respite of a kind to commuters who face uncomfortable journeys of one and a half hours to and from work. Further out still, in what remains of Tokyo's rural hinterland, the silence and darkness in the evenings are near total. Every spring, as yet safely beyond the steadily encroaching sprawl, farming families fly giant carp bunting in anticipation of the Boys' Day festival and perhaps also to celebrate their escape.

Similar urban transformation has occurred throughout Japan. Indeed, practically the entire narrow eastern coastal strip from Tokyo down to Hiroshima is in danger of becoming one contiguous built-up zone. It is not a pleasant prospect. The constant employment of standardized wood-board and plastics has left many areas, without the urban traditions of a Tokyo or Osaka, a wasteland. Seemingly uncontrolled development – without the slightest aesthetic pretence – has achieved little more than a series of miniature Ginzas for the enjoyment of newly urbanized citizens living in quickly made and easily demolished flats and houses. Japan as its tourist information offices might wish it to be has largely disappeared.

The late 1980s saw Japan firmly set on a vast, unprecedented, spending spree that further denuded the natural environment. Large sections of Tokyo were left with almost no open spaces or recreational areas as the smallest patches of unused land and the few remaining orchards were bought up and promptly built upon. Excess liquidity in the banking system generated a huge surge in stock market and property prices that, in turn, persuaded seemingly staid corporate accountants to join in what Japan's media simply termed 'the money game'. Foreign journalists for their part were expected to report with disbelief on the extraordinary price of imported consumer goods and to offer quick calculations on the astronomical cost of a few square metres of real estate on the Ginza. The world was told incessantly that the Imperial palace grounds in the heart of Tokyo were worth more than the entire state of California.

This was Japan's South Sea Bubble. Prices rose regularly without the slightest basis on anything remotely related to economic fundamentals. It was a short era of extraordinary greed and a frenzy of consumption. Once previously unobtainable luxury items were suddenly within the reach of the middle classes. Those who had already made their fortunes on the rising markets promptly flew to Hawaii and California to purchase virtually any housing that took their fancy, while in New York Mitsubishi went a stage further and invested in that American icon – the Rockefeller Centre. Sony too disturbed American opinion by successfully bidding for Columbia Pictures in 1989. The Japanese appeared to be buying up all things American thanks to their bottomless money bags.

Prophets predicted that the sky was the limit for the future of the Japanese economy. Projections based on these boom years encouraged the Japanese people to anticipate the moment when the size of the Japanese economy would shortly exceed that of the United States in absolute terms, though Japan, of course, had already won a higher average per capita income. For one brief moment in April 1995 the surge of the Yen (to seventy-nine to the dollar) did indeed bring this rather empty triumph, but by then Japan had too many of its own domestic problems to start rejoicing. Some Western financial commentators cautioned against taking these new claims too seriously, however, particularly as on a purchasing power parity basis Japan was still considerably poorer in terms of international comparisons than its opinion makers would have it imagine.

The sudden bursting of the Japanese 'bubble economy' in 1990 left a trail of disaster in its wake. Professional reputations were savaged by the new realities of stock market falls, and emergency property sales were conducted at almost any price around the globe to ward off the bankruptcies that threatened Japan once credit was tightened. French Impressionist paintings that had been bought for ludicrously inflated prices at the height of the boom (Christie's had auctioned Van Gogh's portrait of Dr Gachet for $83.9 million, the highest price ever paid for a work of art) had now to be sold off ignominiously for a fraction of their recent cost. The after effects of the bubble years have still to be solved a decade later. In January 1998, for example, it became necessary for the Ministry of Finance to admit that Japanese banks held thirty-five trillion Yen of bad loans when employing US standard accounting. On the same morning shares in the collapsed Yamaichi securities firm were being quoted at one Yen on the Tokyo stock exchange. The Yen itself has slumped to 133 Yen to the dollar, reflecting the unsatisfactory state of the economy. Property values have yet to recover and the prices on the Tokyo stock exchange remain far below the levels reached a decade ago. The entire banking sector is in considerable difficulties because of profligate mangement and the inability to collect vast nonperforming loans taken out during the boom years.

In the spring of 1998, despite a succession of emergency economic measures intended to restore public confidence in the battered financial system, Japan's prospects still remained at best uncertain. When compared with the heroic post-war age or even the more modest growth after the 1970s, the nation was clearly disappointed at its performance. The vigour and self-confidence of the past has seemingly disappeared. The loss of this vitality leads many in Japan to fear that the future may well belong to other states. While it may make economic sense to suggest that all economies must inevitably mature and face the realities of declining growth rates, such arguments offer cold comfort to a nation that had become very used to viewing itself through comparative statistical tables. Since there is not yet an alternative to economism on offer, the public is ill-prepared for what are likely to be further unpleasant events in the new century. The discomfort ahead is likely to lead to higher unemployment rates and a call for more urgent and comprehensive financial and economic reforms. It is doubtful, however, if the nation's political and bureaucratic leaders have sufficient courage to institute any substantial programme of deregulation that, coupled with taxation cuts, might yet resuscitate the faltering economy. The alternative of piecemeal tinkering is seen as the more probable and less effective road ahead. The rest of Asia and the other G-8 nations can be relied upon to continue to call for greater political courage from Japan, though it is unlikely that these outside voices will carry much weight with a government that fears the electoral consequences of disturbing the status quo. Japan remains becalmed and disheartened.

4

Minimalism: hesitancy abroad

[The] Emperor had said he deeply appreciated how much military and economic assistance of the United States had meant for Japan's survival in [the] post-war period and that he hoped for continuance of this assistance. He desired that Japan's relations with the United States would remain close and was fully appreciative [of the] value thereof to both countries.

Emperor's comment, February 1956

Japan has earned itself a reputation for being a thoroughly egocentric country, interested only in its own welfare, and yet its continued well-being or even existence depends on international cooperation and trust.

Edwin Reischauer, 1990

Japan is a major international power. Its formidable economic and financial position guarantees Tokyo considerable influence around the globe. The presence of Japan's prime minister at the regular G-8 meetings, the ranking that Tokyo enjoys on financial institutions such as the IMF and World Bank and the fact that the nation is both the largest creditor nation with massive foreign reserves and the leading contributor to international aid programmes are testimony to its hard won status. There are tensions though between the

93

aspirations of its political and bureaucratic spokesmen and the widely held reservations of others at home and among its Asian neighbours that leave the nation unable to act with the clarity or confidence of its European and Asia-Pacific rivals. Japan's relatively low military posture, its limited cultural diplomacy and the hesitancy of domestic opinion continue to reduce its overall impact. This may be changing as the Japanese government has been obliged to reconsider its nation's role in world affairs with the end of the Cold War and the fading of the previously favourable, if asymmetrical, geopolitical and economic relationship with the United States. This had permitted for two generations a remarkable dependency by Japan on Washington in the critical areas of security and trade and led, as we shall see, to Tokyo being able to reap enormous advantages. More recently, under prompting from the United States, the Japanese establishment has begun to discuss the possibility of increasing the nation's future military, diplomatic and economic options. Yet, as Foreign Minister Watanabe Michio acknowledged in April 1993, there remains a disturbingly large gap between 'the role Japan should play' in constructing 'a framework for peace and prosperity' and 'public understanding of the trends of the international situation as well as of Japan's diplomatic activities'. While Japan is not likely to become a nuclear power, it is seemingly set on creating a larger and more articulate exernal policy, though there remain serious historical impediments to this objective. The fact that as late as January 1998, Prime Minister Hashimoto thought it politic to address a public letter to Prime Minister Tony Blair of Britain for publication in the tabloid newpaper with the largest mass circulation on the subject of Imperial Japan's misbehaviour towards prisoners of war in the Far East is indicative of the distance that has still to be covered. Many in

Asia also continue to express distrust of Japan on the grounds that it has neither adequately apologized for its past deeds nor resolved the divisions within Japanese society on how to view its past imperialism. We shall look here at how Japan's post-war foreign relations have evolved since 1952 and assess the possible direction of future Japanese diplomacy into areas that have been seen to date to be either the preserve of the United States as the world's only hegemonic power or the jealously guarded terrain of the five permanent members of the United Nations Security Council.

We will have to be careful not to overstate our case. Japanese foreign policy initiatives since the war have been more noted for their absence than novelty or frequency. If major change is likely to emerge, it follows, therefore, that a number of deeply embedded attitudes (termed by some as 'taboos') will have to be scrapped. In the spring of 1998 it is much easier to identify the reservations that continue to exist than to note the willing acceptance of fresh international responsibilities. The present near decade-long era of economic discomfort has inevitably forced the Japanese elites to concentrate on more pressing domestic issues and increased the temptation to leave awkward questions over the future leadership of Asia or the maintenance of the international political economy to others. The 1990s, with some important exceptions, such as the Japanese role in the reconstruction of Cambodia and recent proposals to extend assistance to the United States in a regional emergency, have not seen the once widely predicted movement towards a Pax Nipponica. The risk today is more of Tokyo's retreat rather than of international resurgence.

First the domestic context. We need to remind ourselves that the Japanese people have not forgotten the Pacific war. The lesson that public opinion has continued to draw from the militarist era is still clear. Some would suggest that this message must inevitably fade in the next two decades but that may be to ignore the ability of families and political associations to recall the war years for younger Japanese. The crescendo of publicity every year culminating on the anniversaries of the atomic bombing of Hiroshima and Nagasaki ought not to be ignored when analysts call for a more rational defence policy and speak of the need to define a comprehensive national security programme for Japan. At the very least it might suggest that some political views should be tampered with only after considerable effort has been made at public persuasion. The contemporary Japanese soldier is not a figure held in high esteem, thanks to the behaviour of his grandfather's generation. (I have yet to teach a single student who would openly admit that he or she was interested in pursuing a career in the Self-Defence Forces (SDF). Japanese universities are replete with centres of peace studies but it takes a brave college president to consent to the establishment of a research institute of military affairs.)

Hatred of war, often without regard to Japan's geographic or strategic position in east Asia, is a strong restraint on any Japanese governmental hopes of increasing its military spending or enlarging its off-shore defence responsibilities. The SDF is more usually seen by the public as an auxiliary unit to be called upon to assist in coping with Japan's frequent natural disasters than a fighting force capable of defending Japan's borders. It is more the image of the soldier as back-up fire-fighter or flood-controller than peace-keeper. The difficulties that the SDF has over recruitment, the reluctance of farmers to cooperate over training and munition storage plans and the wall of hostility it must attempt to surmount in explaining its mission to a sceptical public remain. This has led to the absurd situation where voluminous government publications on Japan's current diplomacy avoid virtually any reference at all to strategic issues beyond a passing note to the US-Japan security treaty and statements such as 'it is important for Japan to continue explaining its defense policy, including its exclusively defense-oriented policy, at every opportunity'.

The strongest evidence against any substantial military build-up is the need for successive Japanese prime ministers (whatever their personal views on defence) to pledge their commitment to restrain military expenditure to approximately 1 per cent of GNP. This is, indeed, a sacred cow. It has grown in importance over recent decades and is regarded by the public as an article of faith. It certainly makes the preparation of a defence budget more difficult and has led to vociferous complaints from the United States. The 1 per cent figure, when combined with Japan's constitutional restraints on expanding beyond self-defence and the government's continuing opposition to Japan's manufacture and possession of nuclear weapons, would appear to limit severely any substantial growth of Japanese militarism now or in the future. There are certainly strains on Japanese pacifism but relatively few of them can be said to originate from the public at large. The Japanese people may be ·oblivious to many present realities of international relations in northeast Asia but they do know only too well what happened last time Japan sought to dominate the Pacific. The seemingly endless foreign concern over if and when Japan might decide to go nuclear is understandable but somewhat unrealistic in the light of the state of Japanese domestic sentiment. It would take major changes in the power rivalries of the region and considerable enlargement of the nuclear club before the issue left the realm of conjecture. Today it is not on the cards.

Japanese public sentiment is one of a number of factors to be considered in any discussion of Japan's foreign policy. The relatively unchanging attitude of the Japanese people – cutting across political allegiance – has proved both a source of consistency and a problem for successive LDP administrations. Having been at peace for the past five decades it would be very difficult to convince the public of the advantages of substantially increased military spending or alterations to the 'peace' constitution of 1947. Japan said good-bye to its expansionist past in August 1945 and is not to be easily tempted to travel down the same road again. The metamorphosis has been too successful for significant political groups to garner support for alternative policies. Japan has no military-industrial complex and the climate of opinion today would be wary of spokesmen who claimed the need for such a development.

All this makes the preparation of a coherent foreign policy fraught with difficulty. Public opinion appreciates only too well the blessings of peace and feels that by remaining a non-nuclear, lightly armed nation it may continue to avoid the conflicts which have been a prominent feature of the post-war Asian political scene. The government's responsibilities have, of course, to take note of far wider and more complex realities. It cannot afford merely to follow the head-in-the-sand approach of public opinion. Yet any strong challenge to the present orthodoxy of limiting Japanese rearmament and stressing the economic dimension of foreign policy is unlikely to achieve the desired results. The media and most opposition parties would create sufficient furor to oblige the government to retract its statements. In Japan change is more often incremental. Gradualism may win where confrontation will fail.

What then are the outlines of contemporary Japanese

external relations and how might they alter in the medium term? The collapse of the Soviet Union, the rise of China and the emergence of a series of Asian economies that have burst rapidly through the successive stages of modernization have drastically altered the international politics of the entire region. Yet the outlines of Japan's external relations have changed far less than might well have been envisaged in the aftermath of the euphoria of the end of the Cold War in 1989. There has been little in the way of any Japanese peace dividend to date. Indeed, it can be argued that the end of the Cold War in the Asian-Pacific region has complicated rather than simplified Japanese security and diplomatic policies, leading to the present debate with Washington over a new division of labour on defence issues. It took six years after the collapse of Communism, for instance, before Japan and the United States could agree on at least the outlines of a revamped security relationship. Even in the spring of 1998 the flesh has yet to be put on these bones and there are still major difficulties over how the public in Okinawa might respond to anything less than the phasing out of the bulk of the remaining US bases on the Ryukyus.

The Japanese Diplomatic Bluebook for 1992 stated that the nation 'assumes an extremely important responsibility and role in securing world peace and prosperity'. A decade earlier the sentiments were more modest, though the belief in 1981 that 'the mission of Japan's foreign policy is to protect liberty and democracy, the basic values on which our nation stands, and to ensure a safe and affluent livelihood for our people' is probably how most citizens continue to regard Japan's external relations today. It is economic diplomacy that matters most for the public, in keeping with the great leap forward of the past half century. To achieve such goals the Japanese government has continued to stress its partnership with the

United States, which was first formalized by the 1952 security pact, and to strengthen its economic ties with the Asian-Pacific region, the Western industrial powers, the Middle East and what was formerly termed the Third World. It has also constantly to keep in mind its geopolitical position in northeast Asia vis-à-vis the former Soviet Union, China and a still divided Korea.

Japan's relationship with the United States is unquestionably 'the cornerstone of its diplomacy'. This apparently unlikely alliance has endured since the occupation and it would be unwise to imagine that the undoubted relative decline in American power in the Pacific region might lead to its future demise. What is more probable is that there will be more strident calls from the United States for a greater Japanese defence effort in the light of continuing uncertainties on the Korean peninsula and the modernization of the previously antiquated Chinese military. Whether Tokyo will respond significantly to approaches from the United States for a determined build-up in its SDF is problematic, given the state of Japanese public opinion. Any Japanese cabinet would be tempted under such domestic circumstances to offer alternative proposals to the United States, which might stress Japan's reservations over reequipping its forces and suggest instead additional economic and technological assistance to supposedly deserving nations.

The US-Japan relationship, despite the past strains over the nature of the security treaty, the particular problems associated with the question of Okinawa and difficulties inherent in the mere American presence through bases on Japanese soil, has survived to embarrass its many opponents. The Japanese hard left, however, will continue to remain unimpressed and critics within the United States will persist in denouncing the arrangement as a 'free ride' for Japan whereby Tokyo gains protection on the cheap. Europeans have by now grown used to hearing the frequent references to what Ambassador Mike Mansfield in the 1980s termed the 'US-Japan partnership' with the claim that this constituted 'the most important bilateral relationship in the world, bar none'. (It would have been intriguing to have heard Mrs Thatcher's response to such harping on about Pacific bonds.) Doubts have long abounded over such sentiments when Japanese public opinion surveys demonstrate great scepticism over being able to rely on American protection should Japan be threatened militarily, and American attitudes towards Japan may be hardening in the light of a return to the problem of renewed Japanese balance of payments surpluses and difficulties over providing alternative sites within Okinawa for consolidating US bases.

Why then has the arrangement, which was undeniably a forced marriage in the 1950s, persisted? Obviously because both governments have found sufficient advantages in the relationship to overlook the faults inherent in any alliance. The scheme has evolved considerably from the days when Japan was poor and uncertain of its future in a hostile environment of Communist neighbours and sceptical ex-enemy nations. Today more is certainly expected from Japan. Prime Minister Nakasone acted forcefully, as we have shown, to earn American goodwill through his public statements on aligning Japan with the West, but demonstrating sufficient resolve to satisfy Washington in the late 1990s is likely to be harder to achieve. The end of the Cold War saw the ending of Japan's privileged position as a silent appendage of the United States but not of the slowness with which its governments in the 1990s have gingerly reviewed the Pacific relationship.

The Clinton administration may be finding the defence of

its allies in Asia an onerous task that it is not prepared to countenance without substantial Japanese assistance. Yet the SDF is hardly capable at present of doing much beyond temporarily delaying any aggression against the Japanese archipelago and must put its faith in the United States coming to the rescue. Even more disturbing is the clear reluctance of Tokyo to articulate what it would do in the case of a major emergency on the Korean peninsula or how it could cooperate in substantially assisting the response of American forces to such an eventuality. The present 'nuclear fiction' that the Japanese government is unaware of the introduction of American nuclear weapons into Japanese waters also leaves the entire debate of what response Tokyo might expect from the United States a non-starter. Much of the discussion in Japanese circles on defence and foreign policy has a similar air of unreality about it. Figures on the left still talk of waving white flags, while the government dislikes doing anything that might give the impression of any weakening of the all-important issue of civilian control. (Sensitivity on this score has ensured that no military figures have a seat on the National Defence Council that advises the prime minister on defence issues.) There is also the difficulty for Japan of balancing its imperative of maintaining the alliance with the United States and working to improve its links with the People's Republic of China. It wishes, if possible, to achieve closer political, economic and now military contacts with Beijing, without antagonizing Washington by supporting its general policy of constructive engagement with China.

The two parallel responses of American irritation and tacit understanding of the domestic background to Japanese foreign policy are likely to persist. Japan has put its trust in the United States since 1952 and, while it may have other options for the future depending on the international situation in east Asia and beyond, it is not about to make any dramatic changes in its basic orientation. It must expect, however, shortly to provide more tangible action over means to cement the alliance. The days when one rationale behind American ties with Japan was to ensure that Japan itself did not once again threaten the Pacific are long gone. The last senior American military figure to comment unwisely on this issue was General Stackpole of the US marines, who was quoted as saying that his men were the 'cap in the bottle' to deter Japan. The United States now is eager for the Japanese Maritime Self-Defence Force to move beyond its coastguard mentality to cooperate in patrolling the sea lanes between the South China Sea and Japanese territorial waters. The deployment of more modern missiles is also being strongly pressed by the Pentagon, and would be taken as encouraging testimony to the fact that the Japanese government is serious about defending its territory. Yet at a time of government budgetary retrenchment in an era of negligible growth, it will take considerable political courage to persist in any prolonged expansion of SDF expenditure. The risk behind such hesitancy, however, is the possibility of an eventual reconsideration of the United States' entire Asian-Pacific strategy. Beyond the grudging commitment to assume at least some greater share of the defence burden is the unspoken but everpresent Japanese nightmare of a largescale American retreat from the region. The United States did after all pull out from the Philippines in 1992 and any Japanese trumpeting of 'our situation is different' deserves to be promptly stifled. Officials with longer perspectives might also recall that the seemingly unbreakable Anglo-Japanese alliance of the first two decades of this century ended up in the gutter. The unprecedented longevity of the US-Japan security relationship is no guarantee of its immortality when we are in what the Japanese Ministry of Foreign Affairs itself defines as an era of historic transition.

The drawbacks to Japan's current defence thinking are echoed in its foreign policy. Much of Japan's post-war external relations have been essentially passive, leading to cynical queries as to whether the Japanese government could be said to have anything worthy of the name of a foreign policy. Its claim to be concerned over East-West and North-South problems has not always been met with quite the applause the foreign ministry might have hoped for, while its statements on its readiness to cooperate with the other advanced industrial nations of the West would win an unsympathetic hearing in Detroit or Duisburg. Even in the midst of the current Asian financial crisis of the late 1990s, it was hard to discern much appreciation overseas for Japan's attempts to support its neighbours or indeed to build up a head of steam to reinvigorate its own ailing economy. Sakakibara Eisuke, deputy finance minister for international affairs, whose influence on the global economy by 1998 has led to him being the only Japanese bureaucrat with both an international reputation and an international nickname ('Mr Yen'), was widely criticized abroad for inaction. Sakakibara might maintain that 'We have the money and we have the ability to solve Japan's problems', but Charlene Barshefsky, the US trade representative, felt that Tokyo's 'efforts to date have been absolutely inadequate' and further cautioned Japan against attempting to revert to its tried and true trade policy of exporting itself out of a slump instead of boosting domestic demand.

Yet, if Japan has remained largely an adaptive power that shifts as international circumstances alter, it has achieved a rare degree of success for a state that prefers to be a minor military nation in an international system based largely on force. Having achieved so much in such a short time, it would be strange indeed if the Japanese public would immediately wish to alter its diplomatic stance merely to satisfy overseas powers. Those who encourage Japan to play a larger role in regional affairs and beyond have first to convince sizable portions of its electorate. The public, unfortunately for some, has been long accustomed to invoking the defensive nature of its undermanned and underequipped military forces and thinks of Japan exclusively as a still vulnerable and friendless economic power standing equidistant between power blocs while seeking to pose a threat to no one. Tokyo's economic and financial might is being deployed rather cautiously overseas at present but many of the southeast Asian nations that are experiencing the consequences of excess liquidity have found Japan generally supportive. It should not be forgotten that no other single state has such a stake in the financial future of the entire region. The so-called 'tiger' economies have relied heavily on Japanese inward investment to propel themselves forward and Japan is certain to remain the leading investor in the Asian-Pacific area. Governments from Jakarta to Seoul must necessarily defer, at least in private, to this abiding economic reality.

Politicians are rarely brave or foolhardy enough to jettison popular policies for the sake of acquiring a larger role, in this instance, in international affairs, unless it can be demonstrated that the exercise is likely to be in its people's own interests. This will not be easy and the LDP may be tempted to risk the wrath of the United States and the European Union rather than comply in earnest. Japan in the Cold War decades had been slow or unwilling to perceive what some saw as an expanding Soviet 'threat' to east Asia. It has likewise been largely unsympathetic to complaints made by co-members of the West's economic summit that it shares a substantial responsibility to assist in rekindling world economic growth. The Japanese public would undoubtedly prefer its government's foreign policy to concentrate on solving domestic economic issues and avoid entangling alliances that might have unforeseen complications. It wants, in effect, the world to ignore Japan's existence as anything more than merely one of a number of similar middle-ranking trading nations. The rest of the world has no intention of permitting anything of the kind. Japan, whether it likes it or not, is a most important factor in the global balance of power and the global political economy. The United States has been unwilling since 1945 to release its hold on Japan, though it would never in the 1980s have used such intemperate language, since Japan was a prize that it continued to deny to the then Soviet Union. More recently Washington has intended to retain close links to Japan at a time when the People's Republic of China has frequently voiced anxieties that the US-Japan security treaty perceives Beijing as a potential adversary. The United States hopes that its non-hostile policy towards the PRC will blunt such fears. The Clinton administration and its successors would not wish to see a Sino-Japanese axis developing in the future from China's ability to wean Japan away from its traditional moorings. It is apparent that Japan's industrial and financial strengths, when coupled with its technological skills and military potential, ensure that its activities will continue to be most carefully monitored and analysed in east Asian capitals and beyond. Although many in Japan would find this perverse, such close attention on Japan's behaviour is a reflection of the nation's regional might and confirmation of its return once again to a position of power among its neighbours and far beyond. The differences, however, between the Imperial Japan of the Greater East Asia Co-Prosperity Sphere and the Japanese economic giant in Asia today need to be underlined. Tokyo wishes to be seen as a non-military state and is careful to offer economic aid and inward investment to the region to counterbalance the easily orchestrated Asian charges of a return to the aggression and exploitation of the Pacific war era.

The economic dimension of Japanese external relations has clearly been the basis of Japan's post-war dealings with the rest of the world. It is unlikely that this rather single-minded approach can be quickly corrected and the rhetoric about Japan assuming a more extensive international role remains suspect. The view of the Japanese public that issues of 'high politics', which traditionally at least have been based on military and political strengths, ought to be the preserve of powers other than Japan persists. This leaves Tokyo to concentrate rather conveniently on 'low politics', where, of course, its economic and financial policies have been particularly effective and Japan's inadequacies in diplomacy and security are of less importance. For the moment then it might be advisable to treat some suggestions that Japanese perceptions of the world have changed with caution. Even the frequently evoked thesis that economic interdependence between nation-states and non-state actors has led towards an unregulated global economy dominated by multi-national corporations and financial institutions is often rejected in Japan, despite the attention given to this thesis by commentators such as Ohmae Kenichi and his claim that major companies are 'denationalizing' as 'money, goods, people, information and even companies crisscross national borders so freely'. Most Japanese opinion continues to see international economics as a competitive zero-sum game

107

between states, and its own authorities naturally are keen to maintain their national controls in the face of a 'borderless world'.

It will also take time for popular opinion to be convinced that the United States' security guarantees to Japan have to be earned, rather than assumed to apply automatically in all circumstances regardless of Japan's own limited military endeavours and the conventional interpretation of the 1947 constitution as prohibiting Japanese participation in collective security arrangements. The idea of Japan as a neutral, trading nation that has departed from the messy world of Realpolitik still applies. The opinions of the left-wing study group that thought in 1950 that 'Japan must firmly maintain the policy of strictly avoiding interference or involvement in any international dispute' continue to be widely endorsed. Innocence has not yet been lost. Moralism, drawn from one strand of the American foreign policy tradition, is far from extinguished. The bloodbaths of post-war Asia tend to be ignored and the dangers of resource scarcity and envy in developing states forgotten. Japan's pre-war insistence on its own 'have not' status does not engender any significant concern for the fate of the newly independent nations of today.

Japan's recognition of its own economic vulnerability is certain to remain an important basis for its foreign policy. Dangerous exposure to international pressure if, for example, another and more serious oil embargo were to be applied by OPEC members could cripple entire sectors of its economy. It is widely claimed that Japan's lack of self-sufficiency in some foodstuffs (rice is an important exception) and its energy and raw materials deficiencies have to be constantly borne in mind when Japan approaches the rest of the world. The supposed fragility of the Japanese economy is never far from the surface in the minds of Japanese diplomats. Is Japan then a 'fragile glass tower'? Are its problems in a unique category that merits special consideration from other states?

Statistical evidence would appear to support parts of what is an *idée fixe* of the Japanese public. The absence of crude petroleum and iron ore, coupled with limited indigenous supplies of coal and natural gas, ensures that Japanese industry must import to survive. Until two decades ago nearly three-quarters of Japan's imports were accounted for by mineral fuels (41 per cent in 1979), other raw materials (20 per cent) and foodstuffs (12 per cent) and even in 1995 five of the ten largest import categories were still petroleum, wood, liquified gas, organic chemical products and coal. The strength of the Japanese economy, however, makes it possible for Japan to gain advantageous long-term contracts with a variety of overseas sources that often reduce the risks that colour much popular thinking. Japan, of course, faces the constant danger of oil disruption from its Middle Eastern suppliers through political turmoil in the region, blockade or conflict along the sea lanes, though it is far from being the only nation with such nightmares. In February 1998, therefore, it came as no surprise to hear statements from the Hashimoto cabinet deploring the possibility of the use of American and British force against Iraqi strategic installations. Any international crisis leading to a scramble for resources would fully test the diplomatic skills of the Japanese foreign ministry and be an accurate gauge of Tokyo's influence in the Middle East.

Economic diplomacy will clearly continue to be a central pillar of Japan's international relations. The nation still depends on imported raw materials for its industrial prosperity and some key sectors of its economy are strongly export-oriented. The need to mollify Japan's trading partners over their current account trade deficits will persist, though Japan has perhaps been fortunate that the burgeoning American imbalance with China in the 1990s has reduced Congressional anger at Japan's own trade surpluses with the United States. A less than confident Europe battered by high unemployment, low growth and political doubts over economic and financial union may also find it difficult to resist pointing the finger at Japan. European and North American disappointments, particularly in the 1980s and early 1990s, at their own economic performances did indeed lead to charges that Japan had broken the international trading rules and reneged on its promises to restrain its exporters. Any return to comparable Japanese trade surpluses of the past on the back of a weaker Yen would once again ignite the same criticisms as a decade ago. It will remain an unenviable part of the work of Japanese embassies in other industrialized nations to explain the realities of Japan's trading position and attempt to correct misconceptions. Yet, in comparison with the disputes of a decade ago, the atmosphere surrounding American-Japanese economic relations is more relaxed, thanks largely to the remarkable improvement in the state of the American economy, the generally lower bilateral trade imbalances and a willingness on both sides to take disputes to international arbitration.

We ought now to return from the broad generalities of international economics and foreign policy to the more mundane issues behind Japan's current diplomacy. It has already been suggested that Japan's dealing with the United States is the focus of Tokyo's external policies. The two principal bones of contention concern strategic and trade issues that may be best discussed separately, although both share certain common features. We need to assess whether

present differences make it increasingly likely that references to Japan as the United States' 'most important single
ally' could shift to talk of Washington and Tokyo as 'economic and political adversaries'. The fact that in 1996
Michael Armacost, former US ambassador to Japan, entitled
the memoirs of his four years in the Tokyo embassy *Friends or
Rivals?* is suggestive. Earlier incumbents could afford to take
a more benign view of American-Japanese relations, whereas
Armacost spoke of 'the current malaise in our bilateral
relationship with Japan' and the Japanese press was quick to
dub Armacost 'Mr Foreign Pressure'.

It does not necessarily help to restrict our discussion only
to bilateral matters. Japan and the United States may well
have divergent views on the nature of the strategic balance
in east Asia and the western Pacific that would inevitably
colour how each state sees the world. Japan appears to prefer
to play down the prospect of an explosion on the Korean
peninsula, much as it had earlier scoffed at Soviet military
build-ups in the region, while the United States has been
anxious to instil a less complacent attitude in the minds of
Japanese politicians and bureaucrats. This may be difficult to
achieve, since any substantial recognition of potential
dangers would inevitably lead to calls for more concerted
Japanese assistance. Recent press accounts of earlier joint US-
Japan military cooperation planning suggest that even the
preparation of Japanese contingency papers for a crisis in
Korea was forbidden because of the political sensitivity this
would inevitably arouse in Japan and on the peninsula. The
complexities of the Korean situation, where South Korea has
more than enough difficulties in 1998 over correcting its
own domestic financial and political troubles and where Kim
Jong Il may shortly assume the presidency of a vulnerable
North Korea and thereby complete the consolidation of his

personal power, leave Tokyo with little choice but to monitor events either through multilateral forums or as an observer on the touchline. Japanese foreign policy is also burdened by a lengthy Russian-Japanese agenda. Aside from the perennial issue of the northern islands, this includes the need for Russian agreement on Japanese fishing in its waters, the interest of Japanese industry in Siberian and Sakhalian development projects and the wish to retain flying rights over Russian territory to Moscow and points beyond. While no longer the ideological opponent in a hostile region, Russia remains a near neighbour of considerable military and industrial power, tantalizingly rich in natural resources. The great unresolved problem of how and when the northern territories question might at some appropriate moment be successfully negotiated remains the constant, nagging factor behind Russian-Japanese ties. It is unlikely that a breakthrough is near. Russian sensitivities to its demotion in the international league tables and the domestic pressures that necessarily limit the bargaining hand of any Japanese premier must unfortunately reduce any hopes of ending one of the region's oldest territorial disputes.

It was, of course, to prevent any possibility of Japan falling under the influence of the Soviet Union that the United States was determined to anchor Tokyo within its camp after the end of the Pacific war. Rumours of any wavering by the United States on the extent of its commitments to Japan inevitably bring into question the entire future of Japanese foreign policy. There have been a number of instances going back to the occupation years when some Japanese felt that the United States might be less than wholeheartedly bound to Japan. Recent public opinion polls suggest that the bulk of the Japanese people are satisfied with the present state of

US-Japanese relations but only a small minority appear to be ready to consider closer ties to Washington. The greatest difficulty with such reasoning from an American perspective is that it ignores the deficiencies in the United States' military posture in the Pacific and the growing number of American complaints about the imbalance of the US-Japan relationship. Yet, though there may well have been a security gap, little was done by Japan in the 1980s to fill it. Aside from voicing the familiar charge of 'free-rider', the United States needed Japan every bit as much as it assumed Japan needed the United States. This is no longer the case, however, and the present Japanese government is now in 1998 attempting to demonstrate that Tokyo accepts the necessity of a more active role in keeping with the Clinton-Hashimoto declaration of April 1996 that bilateral policy coordination and security cooperation be accelerated.

If the likelihood, however, of the security issue being solved to the satisfaction of the Pentagon is still problematic, how may we assess the other key factor in the relationship? Until the remarkable upsurge in the American economy and the correspondingly disappointing performance in this decade by Japan, the trade issue had long remained a domestic hurdle for each and every American administration. A decade ago it appeared that the trade gap would continue to grow year after year, bringing in its wake the inevitable political problems associated with Japanese penetration into those areas of the American economy, such as the automobile and electrical goods sectors, where Toyota and Sony have long found a ready market. Currently one quarter of all Japanese exports are destined for the United States and, while it is certainly true that Japan's largest source of imports is the United States, most of this trade is accounted for in primary products. Japan, for example, imports only a handful of American cars annually (less than 50,000 units in 1997), though some European motor manufacturers have demonstrated that exporting to Japan can pay, whereas Japan currently possesses 31.2 per cent of the American passenger car market through selling 3,560,000 cars. How then should the lingering trade disputes between Japan and the United States be resolved? Is it indeed sensible to discuss international economics on a bilateral basis?

It would certainly assist the Japanese case if a global view of Japan's trading position could be introduced into the public debate, but politicians facing reelection can hardly be expected to find their constituents enamoured by the idea. While it may be demonstrable that American consumers have gained by enhanced competition and improved quality brought about by the introduction of Japanese goods, it is also undoubtedly the case that certain American industries have been damaged by Japan's success. Trade associations and trades unions have the political power to resist these developments. The agreement to limit the exportation of Japanese cars to the United States was one important example of Japanese manufacturers being prepared, if reluctantly and under strong pressure from the state, to recognize the dangers of overkill, as was the politically wise decision to begin the making of its cars on American assembly lines. The slow and controversial opening up of Japan's rice, beef and citrus fruit markets was further evidence that even the politically powerful farmers and their LDP backers could be called to heel. Yet there can be little doubt that it took a lengthy period of dreary and bad-tempered negotiations before Japan was ready to alter some of its ingrained trading practices. No doubt, the United States may have overstated the case for the prosecution and conveniently ignored its record of protectionism in the nineteenth century but the results have been beneficial for the urban consumers of Japan. Few dispute that without this foreign pressure there would have been little incentive for first the LDP and then the coalition governments of the early 1990s to accept the process of trade liberalization.

Until approximately a decade ago, in the popular American view at least, the United States was on the receiving end of a carefully controlled series of export promotions that were held to be destroying American jobs. (The fact that the State of California, in particular, has received a considerable boost in employment through Japanese investment is invariably overlooked.) The problem was exacerbated by an even firmer belief that the Japanese market has both formal and informal trade restrictions that have conspired to prevent American manufacturers from gaining a fair opportunity to sell their goods within Japan. The prevalence of such views is unlikely to be diminished by periodic official announcements on new measures to expedite Japanese imports. A series of similar much-heralded measures has left considerable doubts as to whether the easing of customs regulations and the removal of non-tariff barriers has in fact occurred. Japanese bureaucrats tend to react to overseas pressure by both pointing out the relatively low level of remaining trade restrictions and simultaneously promising to correct what one must assume to be formidable non-tariff barriers. The seemingly endless saga of the difficulties involved in persuading Japanese organizations to permit the import and purchase of American-made metal baseball bats was but one trivial example of widespread 'buy Japanese' attitudes. While such public behaviour has, of course, its counterparts overseas, it is not easy to explain the persistently low level of finished goods imported by Japan. It is hard to imagine that in all cases there is a superior or cheaper Japanese substitute.

Attempts to redress the trade imbalance will take much more than mass imports of baseball bats and Californian oranges. What presumably is required of the United States is a shift in business attitudes to meet greatly increased Japanese competition. Statistics tell part of the story. The commitment by Japanese companies in establishing local offices in the United States has rarely been matched by an equal American investment of money and manpower into the Japanese market. The track record too of American firms in Japan is hardly comparable to the Japanese triumphs in the United States. The fact that Toyota is one of the three largest car makers in the world is particularly galling to Detroit and the American psyche. Japan exported fewer than 2,000 cars in 1960 to the United States, yet by 1980 it was sending 1,820,000 cars and by 1997 was celebrating a record year of overseas sales. Japanese engineers have also taken on and seemingly defeated the United States in some semiconductor products. All this has prompted a vast array of American reactions. Some observers have called for a strengthened bureaucracy better organized to fight off the Japanese challenge, while others have preferred to complain at the allegedly improper collusion between Japanese business and government. Japan's advantages, such as a willingness to adopt a long-term view and to cultivate a market without expecting an immediate return on investment, will continue to pay off. Critics who voice doubts about Japan's non-tariff barriers, the undervaluation of the Yen and Tokyo's encouragement of export drives to compensate for slack domestic demand may well score debating points but fail to stop the behemoth.

The problems facing American-Japanese relations are formidable. Major differences over Pacific security and a sizeable Japanese current account trade surplus with the United

States persist. Changes over what the Japanese government might consider to be a larger, more appropriate defence role and measures to correct the trade imbalance will continue into the next century. Indeed there are not a few American pessimists who predict little from the Japanese beyond purely verbal agreements that Tokyo ought to redefine its international responsibilities and vague commitments to take unspecified action to prevent an increased trade surplus.

Where then does this leave the two Pacific allies? All alliances are ultimately marriages of convenience and we must assume that the two nations will continue to regard each other as vital trading partners that have equally important stakes in Asian regional stability. It follows therefore that their differences will damage but not ultimately disrupt their friendship. At times when American congressmen are calling for domestic-content legislation and Japanese farmers are resisting American agricultural imports this will appear to be an act of faith. Yet the consequences of any serious break are probably sufficiently dire to induce a cautionary note that may prevent any lasting damage to the international system. We must hope so.

If Japan's relations with the United States have improved, Tokyo's dealings with Moscow remain permanently strained. The causes are many and they tend to more than counterbalance the interests of those Japanese fishermen and businessmen who remain anxious for Russian cooperation. The historical explanation for Japanese and Russian wariness is understandable. Imperial Japan fought against Russia on four occasions from the Russo-Japanese war of 1904–5 to the Siberian intervention of 1918–22, the border skirmishes of 1938 and 1939 at Changkufeng and Nomonhan and finally the short seven-day war at the fag end of the Pacific war. The

Soviet drive on Japanese troops in Manchuria contributed greatly to Japan's decision to surrender in August 1945 and was seen by the Red Army and naval commanders as the wiping of the slate for the defeats of the Russo-Japanese war. Khrushchev pointed out in an interview with the *Asahi Shimbun*'s editor in 1957 that those in Japan who continued to criticize the Soviet Union for abrogating its neutrality pact with Japan in 1945 might care to recall the undeclared attack by Imperial forces on Port Arthur at the start of the Russo-Japanese war.

At the heart of the many differences between Tokyo and Moscow lies the unresolved question of the northern islands. Japanese claims to the islands are based on nineteenth-century treaties with Russia and arguments that the Soviet Union misunderstood the Potsdam Declaration and San Francisco Treaty. Failure to reach agreement on the fate of the four islands (Habomai, Shikotan, Etorofu and Kunashiri) comprising, in the Soviet and subsequently Russian view at least, the southernmost part of the Kurile island chain has prevented Japan and Russia from signing a peace treaty. The decision of Prime Minister Suzuki to designate 7 February as 'northern territories day' and the incorporation of anti-Russian passages in the annual Defence White Paper were indicative of the government's wish to reinforce public opinion over what most Japanese regard as Russian intransigence. Past statements by Russian officials, such as the one made by its ambassador to Japan that his nation had no spare territory to give away, have not helped placate Japan. The subject came nearest to possible solution during the peace negotiations held in London and Moscow in 1955–6, but the offer of two of the four islands by Moscow during a confused period of intra-party struggle was rejected by Hatoyama. The eventual normalization of relations between

Japan and the Soviet Union occurred in October 1956, when the Japanese government's hopes of gaining a fishing agreement, Soviet approval of Tokyo's admittance to the United Nations and the repatriation of the remaining Japanese internees and prisoners of war held in the Soviet Union were realized. Yet the northern island dispute has dragged on, preventing the conclusion of a formal peace treaty. Prospects for any future settlement of the territorial question are dim.

Broader nationalistic and strategic differences have also contributed to this worsening of Japanese-Russian relations. Having regained Okinawa in May 1972 from the United States, it was certain that Japanese attention would focus on its irredentist claims to the northern islands and their rich fishing resources. Were Japan ever to repossess the islands, the strategic balance of the area would immediately shift since Tokyo and Washington might then be able to blockade the Tsugaru strait and bottle up what remains of the Pacific fleet at Vladivostok. Wider factors are also at work to foreclose any possible solution to the territorial deadlock. The Soviet invasion of Afghanistan in 1979 and the imposition of martial law on Poland in 1981 were denounced by the Japanese government, as was the Soviet threat in 1983 to redeploy any SS20 missiles withdrawn from eastern Europe to its Asian borders. The Japanese foreign ministry was only too well aware that the region might end up as the atomic dustbin for an arms control agreement restricted by both superpowers to Europe only. The reality of Russian power, whether expressed militarily through its blue-water naval build-up and the shooting down of a Korean Airlines aeroplane in September 1983 off Sakhalin, or politically by its influence on developments in Indochina and Korea, inevitably weakens the fading calls for Japanese-Russian cooperation. Unfortunately for both sides, the years since the decline of Communism have not produced the opportunities that many Japanese once eagerly anticipated nearly a decade ago.

If Japanese-Russian relations appear destined to remain stubbornly cool, what may be said of Tokyo's contacts with Beijing? Is it possible to see here a gradual embrace at the expense of the United States and Europe, drawing on the sentimental and cultural links between Japan and a greater civilization? How permanent should one expect the improvement in Sino-Japanese relations to be?

Our starting point for this brief survey will be Prime Minister Tanaka's visit to Beijing in September 1972. He went, to the accompaniment of a fanfare of publicity and impressive opinion polls, to establish diplomatic relations with the People's Republic of China. It was the second act of a 'diplomatic revolution', following closely on the Kissinger-Nixon decision to go to Beijing that had supposedly disturbed the Japanese government and set off alarm bells on the merits of the US-Japanese alliance. Yet relations between Japan and China – symbolized by a 'panda boom' among young Japanese – have not always followed the optimistic path predicted in the months after normalization took place. Japan had been careful not to give offence to the Soviet Union by participating in any triple entente between Tokyo, Washington and Beijing that might have had military overtones and Japan's trading links with Taipei were not sundered.

Japan's return to diplomatic relations with mainland China did not mean the end of the two-China policy that had characterized its dealings with the rival Chinese regimes during the past thirty years. Japan, for all the American pressure associated with the Yoshida letter (whereby the premier promised to have no truck with Beijing) and the consequent April 1952 peace treaty with Nationalist China, had long endeavoured to keep its options open and avoid excessive kowtowing to the United States. Yoshida had made public his views on the subject in January 1951 when he wrote in the American journal *Foreign Affairs* that 'Red or White: China remains our next-door neighbour. Geography and economic laws will, I believe, prevail in the long run over any ideological differences and artificial trade barriers.' This process has continued since the normalization of relations and the eventual signing of a Sino-Japanese treaty of peace and friendship in August 1978. Tokyo, however, has no wish to lose its valuable commercial and financial ties with Taiwan or enter into a tight relationship with the People's Republic of China, since any such action towards one could only antagonize the other. War guilt, appreciation of Chiang Kai-shek's attitude towards occupied Japan (his government renounced its reparation claims) and personal and economic ties with Taiwan had to be balanced after 1952 against those within the LDP and the opposition parties who favoured links with the People's Republic. Although public opinion by 1972 was overwhelmingly in favour of normalizing relations with Beijing, 75 per cent of those polled expressed regret at the severance of diplomatic relations with Taiwan. A similar ambivalence has persisted. Tokyo would be cautious over getting involved in any future Chinese-Taiwanese dispute, where its American and Taiwanese friends would stand in opposition to China and Japan could then be expected to take sides.

Japan's own freedom to manoeuvre is clearly limited, though events since 1952 have already demonstrated where its ultimate objectives lie. Tokyo would like to improve its already amicable contacts with China, to whom it has granted considerable loans and launched teaching programmes as part of its growing cultural diplomacy, and from whom it has expectations of engineering orders and oil-exploration contracts, but this has to be seen within the context of more pressing US-Japanese relations. Although Japan's foreign policy priorities are unlikely to shift, it will press for closer ties to Beijing. The Japanese government and its industrial supporters have repeatedly informed the People's Republic that it is eager to assist in China's modernization and its successes can be seen in the fact that Japan is China's largest trading partner. Japan has no desire to build up the SDF to a level that might rekindle earlier Chinese fears, but it is unlikely to be a comfortable realignment. The most appropriate way forward may be for the United States, Japan and the PRC to work more constructively in multilateral forums where each side could gradually demonstrate its goodwill and encourage the exchange of senior political and military personnel. Confidence-building measures when coupled with deepening three-way trade and financial ties may work to erase the suspicions and hostilities of the past.

For the moment it is apparent that Sino-Japanese relations are relatively warm in comparison with the frigidity of Russian-Japanese contacts, but those engaged with international relations have to bear in mind the future possibilities and potential of a nuclear-armed and industrializing China. A legacy of past estrangement, ideological and human rights differences and divergent economic systems might not be easily overcome, despite much public stress on cultural similarities (only a handful of Japanese speak Chinese in reality) and promises to expand joint developmental projects. It would be premature to anticipate any permanent relaxation until the larger regional configurations are clearer. As one former Japanese official noted in April 1997, 'Of course, China is not our potential enemy, and Japan and the United

States have to make the utmost effort to keep a good relationship with Beijing, but at this moment, nobody knows if China can maintain its stability 10 years or 20 years from now.' Harada Koichi also stated that 'frankly speaking, the most important reason that the US government maintains its current presence is to cope with China's power, which is rising economically, politically and militarily'.

There are other threats to Japan's security that also require mention. The most important of these concerns the Korean peninsula. Here massive military forces that were built up under rival superpower sponsorship face each other in a divided land. Japan's own relations with South Korea have been uneasy (not surprisingly in the light of Japan's colonial past), and because of the Cold War alliance structures in northeast Asia, Tokyo could only begin negotiations in late 1990 with North Korea to establish diplomatic relations. The question of eventual Korean unification must inevitably concern Japan as a near neighbour, as does the more immediate possibility of conflict on the peninsula, stemming perhaps from desperation in Pyongyang if its regime faces economic meltdown. The problems also clouding Japanese-South Korean relations are many. The legacy of imperialism has left both the Korean and Japanese publics ill-prepared even now for any substantial meeting of minds (relations were not normalized until 1965) and the future may be equally difficult at times. For the Japanese government, a reduction of tension on the Korean peninsula would be a blessing, but any unilateral moves by the United States (President Carter was persuaded to change his mind over promised troop withdrawals) would be strongly resisted. Japan's economic interests in South Korea are now substantial, though there are frequent complaints from the Korean side over the predatory attitudes of Japanese capitalism and the unwillingness of Tokyo to provide sufficient investment to boost further what in the last decade has become an industrial rival. The recent financial mess in South Korea has elicited contradictory comments from within Japan, as some view the resulting slowdown as welcome relief, while others admire the determination and unity displayed by Korea in making sacrifices for the recovery of the nation. Such pride is absent from Japan today.

Japan and Europe have not made a success of their post-war relations. Despite attempts at the highest level to strengthen ties and talk warmly of a Euro-Japanese political partnership in the 1990s, there remains a great deal of lost time to be made up before some of the rhetoric can be realized. The titles of recent versions of these events make it apparent that the story is one of 'misunderstanding' or alternatively 'conflict and cooperation'. Neither the Europeans nor the Japanese ought to be satisfied with what has frequently been a bad-tempered and disappointing series of trade wrangles with little attempt to identify shared interests and values. Even in 1998, when some felt there had been substantial improvement in the links, it was hard not to miss the barely disguised delight that Europeans displayed on learning of the latest mishaps to the Japanese economy.

European views of Japan in the early post-war days were far from complimentary. Memories of the Pacific war and fears of a repetition of trade practices employed in the 1930s were the backcloth to Japan's reemergence as an international competitor. European attempts in the 1950s to exclude Japan from GATT were not to be easily forgiven or forgotten by senior Japanese diplomats and trade negotiators later. Undoubtedly these mutual suspicions have left an unfortunate legacy that could be resurrected by politicians and journalists who wished to depict Japan as an unprincipled trader that hid behind its island moat while plotting the death of European machine tools, cars, motorbikes and electronics industries. While the Japanese knowledge of even the larger members of the European Union (EU) is not always as substantial as some apologists would maintain, it is undoubtedly greater than that held by many Europeans of Japan. Any British ambassador to Tokyo must find it difficult to explain to his hosts how a majority of his countrymen apparently still regard Japan as an appendage of China, peopled by low-wage earners whose government has long possessed nuclear weapons. Image here equals unreality.

A collective European image of Japan today can only be guessed at. It might incorporate karaoke singalongs, super-express trains, the death of Mishima Yukio, the novel *Shogun*, Mount Fuji, smog in Tokyo, Japan's determination to hunt whales and the phrases 'economic animals' and 'rabbit hutches', Toyota cars and the Siam-Burma railway. It is largely a combination of technological accomplishment, doubts over the price the Japanese people have had to pay for their economic success and snippets of history. If we add the names of Japanese multimillionaires such as the Tsutsumi brothers, Pearl Harbor, the bomber 'Enola Gay' that destroyed Hiroshima, General MacArthur's direction of the occupation and memories of the Atsugi and Yokosuka bases to our list we have perhaps a comparable American picture. In both cases the image is one of economic tensions and respect underpinned by earlier military confrontations. The forcible opening of Japan by the West in the nineteenth century and later disadvantageous trading and immigration arrangements imposed on Tokyo are quite forgotten. The fact too that Tokyo was already the largest city in the world by the eighteenth century and that Japan clearly possessed a considerable pool of talent on which to draw in its later efforts to modernize at speed are also overlooked when accounting for the rise of Japan.

The United States and Europe, however, have very different approaches towards improving their relations with Japan. At present the United States sees its ties with Japan as possessing a wider dimension than those between the EU and Japan. President Reagan's visit to Japan in November 1983 and later journeys by Presidents Bush and Clinton were all intended to demonstrate to the Japanese people the importance that Washington places on Tokyo as a 'global partner'. This hands-across-the-Pacific attitude is in sharp contrast to Japan-Europe links. Headlines over racist remarks by France's Edith Cresson on the work habits of the Japanese nation contrast poorly with American presidents appearing before the Japanese Diet to deliver speeches that ignored the bitterness of the past in order to concentrate the better on the future. The lack of a unified EU approach to Japanese questions only reinforces such tendencies and permits Japan quite legitimately to play one European state off against another and dilute the possible impact of Union-wide directives or strategies.

Attempts to widen EU-Japanese contacts through increased cultural and personal visits may gradually remove some of the existing European prejudices in circulation. Foreign journalists in Tokyo cannot always help to rectify the situation. They are obliged to file almost incessant economic stories that concentrate on the problems of simplifying import procedures or the latest monthly export statistics but largely ignore Japanese political or social issues. Certainly there is considerable respect for Japanese products but as yet little awareness of how Japanese factories operate or what impact Japan aspires to have on the wider world. The first priority undoubtedly is to improve the strained economic links, but until the continental European economies begin to emerge from their present condition of very high unemployment this is likely to remain a major challenge. Only after the economic dimension has been repaired, should one expect progress over broader political and cultural questions. The best way forward would be to see still more Japanese inward investment in Europe as this both demonstrates Japan's industrial confidence in the nations selected and makes possible a two-way learning process for all involved. Local communities in Wales, Derbyshire and northern France, for example, have been quick to welcome Japanese car manufacturers and electronics makers, knowing that areas of high unemployment badly need this type of overseas commitment.

The language gap between Japan and the rest of the world is unlikely to be bridged. The drawbacks of an education system that stresses abstruse grammatical points but neglects to attend to spoken English, and the scarcity of Japanese-speakers in the West have produced what has been aptly termed a Himalayan barrier to understanding. The only recourse would seem to be through greater use of translations. Purists would prefer to see improvements made in Japan's foreign language training methods and encouragement for Western students to persevere, but neither state of affairs is probable. Most Western readers interested in Japan will continue to rely on translations for their appreciation of the Japanese novel and subtitles for their enjoyment of the Japanese cinema. It may be second best, but then how many people in Britain or the United States read Kafka or Dostoyevsky in the original? The onus will remain on the skilled specialists to provide an accurate account for the large Japanese audience interested in Western thought and behaviour and the much smaller Western group prepared to look at a culture that remains very much on the fringes of most school and university curricula.

What is the current Japanese world view? Where does it place the United States and Europe? What images do the Japanese people hold of the non-Western world? In Japanese eyes the parts of the world that count are limited. Historically the three main models for influencing Japanese institutions and behaviour have been China, nineteenth-century Europe and, since 1945, the United States. The rest of the world may have considerable economic importance to Japan but this has not always led to any great understanding. The photographs of the heads of state and government taken after the annual advanced nations summit best characterize Japan's progress and enhanced self-esteem. The Japanese premier has gradually moved from hanging around on the very edge of the group portrait to being one of the central figures. This recognition by other Western states is what Japan is after. It wishes to see itself and be seen by others as a power worthy of respect. Prime Minister Nakasone, for example, was able to stress Japan's improved status by receiving the German chancellor, the American president and the secretary-general of the Chinese Communist Party as official guests to Tokyo in the autumn of 1983. Cynics were quick to point out that such events carefully coincided with the forthcoming general election, but this need not detract from the undoubted improvement accorded Japan on the world stage. Occasions, such as in July 1993 when Japan in its turn hosted the annual G-7 summit in Tokyo, are necessarily seen as of particular importance. Japan remains the only Asian member of the (now) group of eight industrial nations club and claims to use such forums to speak on behalf of fellow Asian nations.

The process of gaining a greater role in global affairs is not complete. Japan's future will lie in further internationalism but there are, as we have seen, powerful domestic voices which would decry military build-ups or greater aid contributions; there are also other states that might oppose any strengthening of Japan's position. Tokyo, however, has met with less resistance than in the past over its determined but yet unsuccessful campaign for a permanent seat on the United Nations Security Council, whereas twenty years ago it was humiliated by losing to Bangladesh in the battle to gain a two-year term as the Asian Security Council representative and, equally disappointingly, Nagoya had to suffer the indignity of seeing the 1988 Olympic games be awarded to Seoul. With Japan's hosting of the winter Olympics at Nagano in February 1998 and its co-hosting of the next soccer world cup with South Korea, there is really no longer any need to bid for such expensive international prestige events. Friendships, however, can be fragile and Japan has few states it can rely on. It may have to work hard to gain Asian and Pacific cooperation; greater sensitivity over its commercial practices and social behaviour might help. More technological assistance not only to ASEAN states (Malaysia, Singapore, Indonesia, Thailand, the Philippines, Brunei, Vietnam, Laos and Cambodia) but to much poorer African nations is called for. Fewer organized sex tours to Bangkok and Manila also would not go amiss.

'Japan is not an immigrant country.' This statement by the director of the Foreign Ministry's division of refugee affairs is a frank and somewhat disappointing commentary on Japanese attitudes towards the rest of the world. Whether the subject is governmental and public resistance to Vietnamese 'boat people', the minuscule interest in support of Amnesty International or opinion polls depicting popular xenophobia, similar wariness emerges. Whatever the historical explanations for such isolationism it is, if only for reasons of Realpolitik, hardly in Japan's interest to perpetuate these attitudes. What might be done to rectify the situation? Or is it sufficient for Japan's dealings with the rest of the world to be restricted to a handful of civil servants and employees of the major trading companies?

We must admit that efforts have been made in the past decade to come to grips with some of the problems. The media and a few politicians have spoken of 'internationalizing' Japan, though the phrase risks being overworked as a substitute for any real action. Government funds have been employed by the Japan Foundation to project a picture of Japan different from the usual diet of balance of payment surpluses, and private industrial foundations have been generous in their support of a few select institutions overseas. Domestic universities and research centres have also been created in an attempt to encourage greater consciousness of the external world. Yet the problems to be surmounted are not solvable merely by such measures, laudable though these efforts may be.

Not much can be done about Japan's history, though deletion from its textbooks of the euphemisms used to describe Japanese aggression in Asia would help, and nothing to alter its geography, but government initiatives might be tried to modify public attitudes. Language instruction in schools could be sharpened up, gestures such as relaxing the nationality laws might be introduced and more attention paid to Japanese aid programmes. None of this is likely to make an instant impression, but it might be received as evidence of a gradual change of heart by overseas audiences. The Japanese picture of the rest of the world unfortunately is a severely hierarchical one that permits little recognition of less developed Asian or African states. It usually accepts North America and western Europe as ageing but respected prize-winners and condemns the remainder of the world to limbo. Given the usual propensities for democracies and their elected representatives to stress bread and butter issues unless facing an imminent threat to their security, it would (once again) be unwise to expect any immediate changes. Japan is likely to remain inward-looking, in keeping with its belief that charity begins and ends at home. The social costs to overseas communities of Japanese exporting prowess are and will be frequently ignored by a public that feels its trade rivals must pull up their socks if they want to remain competitive. Foreign relations will probably still be largely a matter of economic diplomacy. If no longer quite the silent power of a generation ago, Japan will persist in keeping its head down. Any increase in Japan's international stock will be gradual.

Discussion of 'Japan's new world role' is possibly premature. Academics and analysts may be jumping the gun when they talk repeatedly of Japan's political and economic responsibilities in a changing international system. Often the domestic context of Japanese politics is glossed over too rapidly as the commentator leaps to present his personal prescription for how Japan ought to behave in a complex world. There is an air of unreality behind parts of the debate, since the evidence suggests that the Japanese public is decidedly wary of much of this appeal to its pocket and conscience. Opinion polls and editorials repeat that Japan is hesitant over expanding its defence capabilities, despite what it sees as an increase in foreign threats to its territory. Russia is regarded as an unfriendly neighbour by many Japanese, while a majority of the public has long doubted whether the United States would protect it in an emergency. The US-Japan Security Treaty takes on a different hue when seen from the perspective of a public that remains sceptical of the value of this link if put to the test. It is improbable that any Japanese government in the foreseeable future would greatly increase defence spending much beyond 1 per cent of GNP. The suggestion that Japanese industry needs to encourage rearmament to fill its order books is implausible.

How then is Japan to provide the means for an enlarged international role? The answer rests on one's assessment of likely Japanese political and bureaucratic responses to the counter-forces of domestic opinion and American appeals. The entire subject has to be conjectural and any guess must be prefaced by acknowledgement of one's ignorance. It may be thought pessimistic by some, but the prospect of Japan taking an active role in the defence of sealanes or providing more than occasional assistance to United Nations peace-keeping forces appears remote. Certainly the extreme hesitancy displayed by Japan during the Gulf war of 1990–1 is no longer likely to be tolerated by the international community and the passage of Diet legislation in June 1992 does provide for the despatch of Japanese civilian and military personnel to United Nations peace-keeping operations, but a pragmatic people sees little benefit to be gained by participating in such uncertain ventures. Japan did not exactly cover itself in glory during its operations with the UN in Cambodia and the probability of it joining any comparable scheme in the near future is remote. Japanese citizens are proud of their pacifist state and prefer that their government offer financial donations as the best means of contributing to multilateralism. This determination to limit its roles has undoubtedly worked against Tokyo's long-held wish to gain permanent membership of the UN Security Council. It would take, however, considerable evidence from unfavourable events in east Asia to shift public opinion. The shooting down by the Soviet

Union of a KAL aeroplane in 1983 was used by the government to justify its existing military expenditure, rather than as a timely opportunity to add to predetermined appropriations. Reminders of Soviet power used to be employed successfully by some as confirmation of the wisdom of retaining a low profile rather than as testimony to support greater militarism. Equally, the wish to avoid antagonizing China in the late 1990s will leave it reluctant to speak out over human rights violations, military incursions or territorial disputes in the South China seas. Relations with Beijing will be the focus of much Japanese diplomacy in the first years of the next century. The Chinese siren song will be loud and clear.

5

Stability: social cooperation and change

A substantial number of women continue to devote their energies, full time, to the home, and these have succeeded in carving out, or perhaps having carved out for them, a role which is widely regarded as a professional occupation.

Joy Hendry in *Japanese Women Working*

The days of corporate feudalism are ending, casting in doubt the future of lifetime employment and seniority-based wages and promotion.

Fujiwara Sakuya, 1997

'I'm optimistic. We have done just fine in the 50 years since the war, and we should proceed with confidence during the next 50 years.' This brisk response of former prime minister Miyazawa Kiichi when asked the standard question on whether Japan in February 1998 betrayed none of the doubts that others mutter in private but are cautious about expressing to outsiders. Miyazawa's show of bravado is unlikely to be matched by society at large, given the host of issues that the nation is obliged to confront in the next decades. Certainly in comparison with the difficulties ahead of regaining a decent economic peformance, coping with an ageing population and providing a better urban environment, it is

134

possible to look backwards with an attitude that risks almost approaching one of nostalgia. Since many at the turn of the century sense that Japan's best days may be behind it, it is tempting to view the past half century as the exceptional era when the nation and the international context were both at their best.

Our sketch of contemporary Japanese politics, economics and international relations may have provided some pointers to Japan's present identity, social structure and values. For all the changes since the Pacific war Japan remains a con-servative, bourgeois and cautious nation intent on retaining the modified institutions that have served it well since the disasters of militarism seemingly wiped out the handiwork of the previous three generations. We shall first look briefly at Japanese self-perceptions.

No other major industrial society has anything ap-proaching the racial homogeneity of Japan. The largest minority group is the Burakumin composed of the descen-dants of outcasts with occupations such as butchers, shoe-makers and junk collectors. Prejudice against the more than two million Burakumin is strong and persistent. The only other sizeable minorities are of Korean and Chinese origin – the number of North American and European residents is minuscule. The population of Japanese nationals in 1996 was 124,709,000, whereas the total of registered foreign residents in the country was only 1,415,136. There is also an unknown number of illegal workers, employed mainly in the construc-tion and entertainment sectors, though the setbacks to the economy recently are likely to have substantially reduced their presence. The small size of non-Japanese groups, which is aided and abetted by the immigration policies of succes-sive Japanese governments, has contributed in a large degree to the uniformity in Japanese social behaviour. History and geographic isolation have been combined with this racial unity to fuel a strong sense of national identity. It is not and will not become necessary in the future for the Japanese to wonder excessively over what constitutes their national character. It is certainly true that the subject holds a fascination for the public but this pursuit may have an element of narcissism attached to it. Countless articles and books have been produced which analyse the uniqueness of the Japanese people. The readers generally believed this before they bought the texts that said what they already knew but wanted to hear again.

What is Japanese man? How does he define himself? At the first level, a Japanese is someone born of two Japanese parents. There have, however, been recent alterations that now permit Japanese women married to non-Japanese to pass on their citizenship to their children. Such changes were necessary once Japan had signed the United Nations female anti-discrimination convention in 1979 and the Diet has passed legislation granting children of non-Japanese fathers and Japanese mothers the right to dual citizenship until they come of age at twenty, when they will have to choose which nationality to retain. Naturalization is otherwise extremely rare. To be Japanese often also implies a strong attachment to the nation and to its successes. Any immediate post-war feelings of racial inferiority have long since disappeared. By the late 1960s, pollsters discovered that very few Japanese still persisted in any deference to the West, while nearly 50 per cent expressed a sense of superiority. Nationalism is strong. It has played a major role in motivating Japan's recovery and is never too far from the surface when accounts are made of the nation's fall and subsequent rise. This 'socio-cultural nationalism', however, is essentially benign and does not lead many citizens to any overappreciation of the state's political and bureaucratic leadership. Given that Japan has been convulsed recently by an almost ceaseless succession of political, corporate and now bureaucratic scandals it is most unlikely that the public is about to entertain any great enthusiasm for its establishment. It concentrates rather on the shared cultural and linguistic heritage of the country, though there are certainly ultranationalist fringe elements which take a much more extreme view of what constitutes the supposed core traditions and values of Japan. Such groups, which are not averse to employing intimidation to gain their ends, have long opposed Communism as an alien ideology and would like to see a return to a pre-war Imperial system with an enhanced status reserved for the throne. Many conservatives remain convinced that the US occupation has weakened the people's attachment to the nation and would like to see more respect accorded to Japan's national anthem and flag as well as the elimination of what revisionists term the current 'masochistic' teaching of modern Japanese history. Other attributes which may make up the Japanese national character – if such a composite picture can be said to have much worth – might include a professed strong sense of family, a very considerable attachment to one's workplace, little sense of religion and perhaps an overwillingness to conform when weighing up possible courses of action. Family pressures on such critical occasions as, for example, the choice of spouse can be intense.

Japan is an overwhelmingly urban society where the bulk of the people are crammed into the narrow coastal belt between Tokyo and Hiroshima. Space is at a premium. Social behaviour under such circumstances probably reflects the need to avoid excessive confrontation with one's neighbours and colleagues. Through past history and present necessity

Japanese society may have placed greatest stress on cooperative group activity at the expense of individual endeavour. Consciousness of hierarchy and loyalty to the family, workplace and nation may take precedence over assertiveness and independence.

The encouragement to conform to group norms is presumably drawn from Japan's agrarian experience. Until recently Japan was largely a rural society where the basic social units were the family and village. Sociologists and anthropologists have suggested that parts of the intended village structure have been transferred onto Japan's modern industrial society. Loyalty to one's own small work-group and its supervisor has parallels with the control that a father or landlord might possess. In both cases the safest course of action may be to conform and identify oneself closely with the group and its fate, thereby gaining protection for oneself and the prospect of promotion with others if the company or one's particular section prospers. This may go some way to explain the factionalism of Japanese political, bureaucratic and industrial circles and also the esprit de corps of rival groupings within organizations. Dependence – some might claim over-reliance – on the group's leader may be the consequence of the persistence into adulthood of common childhood attitudes. The giving of presents to one's professor or manager at mid-summer and the end of the year emphasizes this vertical relationship and implies a request for goodwill, in the tradition of the peasant entreating his landlord for protection. This exchange of gifts on numerous occasions has and will continue to link members of society in a series of often tight and at times uncomfortable relationships. It is also the perfect disguise for a great deal of outright bribery.

By European standards Japan is not quite the small nation that its citizens are intent on projecting overseas, since it is larger than Germany, Britain or Italy. In comparison with the United States, of course, it appears in a very different light, though even then if superimposed on a map it stretches from Vermont to the Bay of Mexico. What appears difficult for Western observers to comprehend is the relative ease with which this vast shift of population from rural to urban Japan has been carried out in the short span of the two post-war generations. Reminders of this transformation are seen every December when Tokyo empties for a few, short days as an extraordinary exodus carries families in exile home to their ancestral roots in Niigata and Tohoku. Once the new year festivities are completed, the media reports hourly on the traffic jams and overpacked trains central to what is known as the U-turn back to the Tokyo-Yokohama conurbation.

Today's Japan is an urban society based increasingly on the nuclear family. The small size of city accommodation and the mass migration from the countryside to the cities are two factors that are making it less common for grandparents to live with their eldest son and his family. (Japan's population density is higher than any European nation with the exception of the Netherlands but below that of South Korea and Taiwan.) There are frequent complaints that today's metropolitan generation is suffering from anomie and would wish to return to the less frantic pace of the semi-rural towns, if not the monotony of village life, but the dislocations and neuroses have not produced any great retreat to the country areas. The Japanese people retain a strong sentimental attachment to their home-towns but rarely go back more than once or twice a year for the summer festival and the longer new year holidays. Urban life undoubtedly has its frustrations and inconveniences, centred on the scarcity and price of housing and the virtual necessity for office workers to commute long distances if they are ever to secure a house or apartment of their own in one of the continually expanding suburbs. Housing is grossly expensive. This is caused, inevitably, by the still high price of land, despite some reductions in the past decade, and the reluctance of those fortunate enough to possess plots in the remaining fringe areas to put their land on the market. Home ownership remains, however, the aspiration of many Japanese for which they are prepared to mortgage their pension rights if necessary.

For many Japanese husbands the work-place takes precedence over the family. The small group comprising one's colleagues within a particular department has a very considerable importance for white-collar workers. One's identity is partially formed through membership of this close-knit group. Salarymen expect to be asked to stay late in the office if the group is under pressure. Evenings are often spent in neighbouring bars in the company of one's work-mates. This inevitably weakens family life. Considerable numbers of Japanese children rarely have dinner with their fathers. Even at the weekend (a term which will require definition later) fathers may absent themselves to show a foreign visitor around or to play golf with customers or colleagues. The frequently employed use of the term 'family service' to describe how husbands regard novel obligations to wives and children at the weekend underscores the difficulties in adjustment for the salarymen.

The company or factory is the focus for the lives of many Japanese. It is not solely that the salaryman puts in long hours there, but he is committed to his work-place in a manner quite distinct from some European or North American behaviour. The employee will almost certainly have joined his company immediately after graduation from university on the understanding that he will devote himself to his particular company for the remainder of his working life. It is rare indeed to resign from one company to join another. Once a worker for Matsushita, always a worker for Matsushita. Having obtained employment with a large or medium-sized company, a young graduate can expect to receive extensive training in management within the organization and at least the prospect of further education overseas or a temporary transfer to an Asian or American subsidiary. He – careers for women are regarded as disruptive to one's own company hierarchy and likely to create friction with firms with which one has business dealings – is on a slowly moving escalator. Obviously not everyone will reach a position of great responsibility within the enterprise but most graduates have the opportunity to progress at least to the foothills.

It may be folly to talk of the Japanese company, but certain characteristics appear to be sufficiently widely shared among the larger enterprises to permit an abstract picture. Aside from standard recruitment practices, whereby new employees commence their careers as part of an annual intake every April amidst considerable ceremony and encouragement from the senior management, companies endeavour still to provide 'lifetime employment' and remuneration based on a combination of years of service and job responsibility. They will also attempt to assist over housing for employees (hostels for bachelors and apartments in company compounds for younger married couples) and offer a large number of fringe benefits. Both the company and its employee have made, in effect, an arrangement that asks more of each side than might be normally expected in the West. The ideal may not apply as frequently as the more rhapsodical accounts would have us believe, but talented managers are not easily enticed away or the less than competent immediately dismissed. Semi-annual bonuses do reflect the company's past sales performance. Enterprises wish to be seen as a 'family' and do make efforts to live up to their responsibilities. The sight in November 1997 of the president of Yamaichi Securities weeping as he apologized for his failure to provide employment any longer for his staff was taken to be excessive by the media in the West but such mass sackings because of a business collapse are very much a measure of last resort in Japan. Redeployment elsewhere within the corporate group or early retirement – suitably sweetened – would be the norm.

Most of the features in our account apply only to the graduate entrants within the larger Japanese companies. Salaries and associated bonuses at banks and finance houses, for example, are regarded as abnormally high by the rest of society today, particularly as many of these institutions are virtually bankrupt and are felt to have lost all public trust. The conditions under which others work can be far less pleasant: blue-collar workers, those employed in subsidiary firms and the temporary staff get a rawer deal. These categories gain fewer benefits from their employer and are regarded as no more than adjuncts to the company for which they may be working. Wages in smaller companies are lower, working conditions are less pleasant and safe, bonuses can be minimal and job security non-existent. Yet, Japan, as may be recalled from our chapter on its economic growth, remains a nation of small businesses and backstreet fac-tories. Dualism lives. Here younger workers are much more likely to vote with their feet and move to another firm that promises higher wages and more overtime. The attempts to provide a company network that might bind the employee to his enterprise are necessarily weaker since owners have no spare funds for such luxuries. Bankruptcy fears rather than plans for company-organized tours (males only) to Bangkok occupy the lives of small bosses.

Yet, despite greater job mobility and a considerably reduced wage-packet in smaller companies, much of the same attitude towards work exists throughout the Japanese economy. Society accepts that work is an activity that requires the giving of one's best, whether one is a middle manager in the Tokyo head office wearing pinstripes and the company badge in one's lapel or a junior worker on the assembly line in the suburban factory wearing the alternative uniform of grey battledress. Although packed coffee shops and pinball arcades may suggest otherwise, one's workplace is something that helps define oneself ('I work for Sony, he's from Matsushita') and the activity is assumed to be socially valuable. Management under such circumstances is different, though not necessarily any easier, than that in the West. Those in authority may well face fewer direct challenges to their decisions but it is assumed by their subordinates that efforts will be made to involve the entire group in the pursuit of the company's objectives. Emotional ties may be stronger and the hours spent in gaining this trust and cooperation can be long. Yet many doubt whether what is presently being disparagingly termed 'corporate feudalism' can easily weather the current economic storms. The enormous physical and emotional demands placed on the salarymen have led to a great deal of dubious corporate behaviour and today's economic climate must inevitably limit the ability of all but the world's best corporations to continue to be able to afford the massive costs involved in maintaining the present structure. Critics also claim that the so-called consultation process has an element of fraud behind it, since the company can ultimately insist on getting its own way, but few managers worth their salt would wish to resort to such heavy-handed tactics. Besides, a well motivated workforce is likely to identify more closely with the company and see the sales targets and production control data as their shared goal with the enterprise. A vertical society that pits one's own company against rival firms has less time for class warfare.

To the Western reader the Japanese company must appear at first glance to be a strange bird. Management by approximate consensus, with age greatly influencing promotion until comparatively early retirement (often at fifty-five to fifty-eight but gradually being extended to sixty or sixty-two) forces one to leave, is clearly not the manner in which most European firms are accustomed to operating. The trend in the West is for reductions in the working week, longer holidays and for pressure to rethink the retirement system. In Japan the reverse has taken place. The work week remains longer for white-collar workers than in most of Europe, holidays are short and acceptance of large amounts of unpaid overtime by all ranks above quite junior staff is common. It also makes much heavier social demands on employees. Such a system has little built-in countervailing power. Trades unions are generally weak and often inhibited by being company-based organizations. (It is not unknown for senior managers to have served in their earlier days with the company union.) Ultimately what saves the system from tyranny is the Japanese social climate that conditions both workers and management over equitable behaviour and knowledge that news of layoffs can do irreparable damage to corporate reputations. Managers generally appreciate how far they can press their rulings, while the post-war booms have made it easier to negotiate wage settlements. Labour disputes are rare outside the somewhat ritualistic spring bargaining season, when white-gloved stationmasters on JR can be seen tearing down posters the moment unionists deface property. Strikes do occur on occasion, but most of the animosity of the occupation period when unions challenged management quite openly has disappeared. Yet it was probably the lessons drawn by companies from the early post-war bitterness that gained wider acceptance of 'permanent employment' and a wage related to the individual's family responsibilities. Public memories may have long faded of the days when Toyota was racked by a lengthy labour dispute in 1950 that nearly brought the company to its knees, but the affair was taken to heart by the management.

Japanese education remains a subject of considerable domestic political debate. It has also been of interest to overseas audiences and readers, as the international reporting of the 1982 textbook issue and the student events of the 1960s demonstrated. Recent American awareness of the problems of public education has led also to increasingly favourable comparisons between the Japanese educational system and those of its industrial competitors. Is such praise warranted? What are the strengths and weaknesses of Japanese education?

The subject is controversial. Writing thirty years ago, one British student of Japanese society went so far as to claim that 'perhaps no other educational system in the world is so continuously and so earnestly fought over'. If tempers have cooled in the intervening period, it remained the case that until recently the Japanese teachers' union (Nikkyoso) had to hold its annual conference under close police protection to prevent mobs of ultra-rightists from physical disruption and attempting to deploy loudhailers to drown out all speakers. Perhaps today, however, the political issues – governmental textbook approval excepted – have decreased as attention has focused on the drawbacks of excessive pressure on university entrance examinees and the heavy out-of-school studying that forms a prominent part of the regime of even junior high school members.

A decent education is crucial to the life chances of young Japanese. Since Japan can be loosely defined as a meritocracy where one's first job after graduation is often one's only one, many Japanese are eager to compete for the undoubted advantages that entry into a prestigious university can bring in terms of career and even marriage prospects. Parental wishes for their sons to aspire to a top-ranking university are inculcated from an early age. Admittance to a good high school is a virtual sine qua non for future success, since without competent teachers and a competitive atmosphere only the exceptional pupil will be able to make it. The failure rate for entrance to the universities of Tokyo or Kyoto is inevitably very high, but it does not deter the ambitious from attempting to reach the pinnacle. Only a few can succeed, while the remainder either try again in the following year or make do with their second or third preferences in a pecking order that students and employers alike recognize. Parallels with the rankings made in Anglo-Saxon academic circles are close.

Like it or not (and many on the right do not), Japanese post-war education has found it hard to shrug off its occupation legacy. One future British ambassador to Tokyo warned during those years that the result was already the importation of a deplorable style of 'Hollywood morality'. Yet the outward design of the American educational reforms has remained largely intact. It is true that the control of education has shifted somewhat but the organization of public education was never likely to move far from the control of the Ministry of Education (Monbusho), even in the heady days of decentralization. The shorthand method to describe the post-war reforms is to note that a unified 6-3-3-4 structure defines the new lengths of education available to pupils from elementary school, commencing at six years of age, to junior high school, commencing at twelve and completed at fifteen, through to three years of high school education and then, for a minority even today, on finally to a four-year university course. Pre-war education had only been compulsory up to the completion of elementary school at the age of twelve; thereafter the pyramid had rapidly narrowed with universities very much an elitist affair admitting only a handful of women students.

The United States' advisers and the GHQ staff in the Civil Information and Education section aimed to democratize both the content and administration of public education. The reformers probably had better luck with their first goal. If the Japan of the 1930s and 1940s had regarded education as a tool in the service of the state, the determined occupation authorities attempted to introduce less nationalistic values and promote a greater sense of individualism and respect for democratic values. Teachers, like other groups in Japanese society, were eager to sail with the new breeze and quickly saw their role as preventing any backsliding by the Japanese establishment. Education became something of a battlefield. This did not prevent it from attempting to cater for an enormous upsurge in demand for instruction that might assist in finding one a niche in what by the 1960s had become an affluent society. More and more pupils elected to stay on longer at school in order better to compete for a more prosperous future.

The results have not been entirely happy. Public high school education can be of a high standard (mathematics, for example, is a subject at which Japanese excel in international merit tables, though Japan is at the bottom of the Asian league when it comes to scores in English language tests), but the goal appears to be more often the passing of examinations than the development of personal abilities and a critical spirit. Universities, for their part, expanded their student enrolments far faster than they were able to provide additions to their faculty or facilities. Horror stories of staff reduced to employing microphones to enable themselves to be heard in vast auditoriums abound. Students under such circumstances are fortunate to be on more than nodding acquaintance with their professors. Such conditions played an important part in student dissatisfaction during the 1960s and have only been partially repaired in the years since. Certainly the government has increased the share of national resources devoted to education in both the public and private sectors, but the discrepancies in budgetary allocation and teaching staff between a select national university and a provincial private college can be vast.

Student attitudes towards their education have inevitably varied, but there is undoubtedly a persistent feeling that university life may provide a moratorium on overtaxing one's intellect. It is as if the heavy pressures to gain admittance to a reputable university and the knowledge that in four years one will have to get back into harness and slog away in a trading company or bank combine to encourage the widespread notion that university life should be a pleasant interlude. College administrators appear to be either unwilling or unable to correct this attitude, knowing that in their students' final year most effort has to be put into the competitive search for future employment. It is not uncommon for highly competent women students at my own university, for example, to attend literally dozens of exhausting job interviews at myriad locations throughout the Kanto region before receiving a single offer of employment.

The Japanese public's sense of unease at some features of its educational structure has grown as the competition for the better high schools and universities has intensified. All political parties when campaigning for general elections are certain to produce their pet solutions for the problems of education. A large portion of the blame must be attributed to parents, who simultaneously complain of the 'examination hell' that their offspring are subjected to and yet insist on ensuring that their children attend cramming schools (juku) and tolerate the rote learning essential for passing the entrance examinations. The system may be absurd but the present is apparently not the moment to jeopardize one's son's future. The public is well aware of the glittering prizes that can await the successful Tokyo University entrant. No wonder the examination results for national universities are carefully scrutinized by parents, teachers and personnel managers. No wonder too that the live television broadcasts announcing the university entrance results are sponsored by the crammers.

Japanese education remains largely centralized and uniform. The proverbial nineteenth-century French minister of education who could reputedly sit at his desk and know what his teachers were all up to at any given moment would feel at home if transported to contemporary Japan. (National schemes for education in Meiji Japan were based on French models.) It is true that there have been a number of experimental schools and private initiatives, but these have tended to be ignored in the fight to attain the treasured university place. This goal has left education less egalitarian as middle-class parents have increasingly been prepared to fund private schools where the tuition is felt to be better geared to this end. The result can be seen in the background of successful Tokyo University entrants. The scramble has now reached even the kindergarten level. Prosperous families work hard at developing contacts that might assist their children in starting off on the right foot at the appropriate elementary school and then continuing along the same conveyor belt. Education – a sphere of family life usually the exclusive responsibility of Japanese mothers – is too important a business to be left to chance.

If the press is to be believed, the spectre of an ageing population is haunting Japan. Prophets of doom are eager to point out that Japan's population profile is rapidly changing as grandparents live longer and their sons and grandsons have fewer children. Some of this talk needs to be put in perspective. It is true that Japanese life expectancy is among the very highest on earth and there will be increased pressure on health services and pension schemes by 2025. It is also a fact that the gradual ageing of Japan will have uncomfortable consequences for Japanese industry and the entire social fabric. Yet Japan's present population is still a relatively young one, with 14 per cent of its people in 1995 over sixty-five years of age in comparison with 17.5 per cent in Sweden, 15.7 per cent in Britain and 16 per cent in West Germany. Demographers contend that by the end of the first quarter of the twenty-first century Japan may have caught up with and perhaps surpassed Europe in its share of retirees, but these can be no more than intelligent guesses based on projections into the future of current trends that have necessarily discounted the possibility of upward changes in the birth rate. It might be better to keep an open mind on all this; even actuaries have been known to nod. Statistical evidence, however, on the increasingly late age at which Japanese women are marrying and having their first child does concern many, who fear that this can only lead to a top heavy and less productive society.

What is already apparent is that the structure of Japan's workforce must change and that some further weakening of family ties is likely as more elderly people live apart from their relatives. Japanese enterprises are facing these issues by asking some of their employees to retire early and by taking on more part-time workers in an attempt to control the escalation in their costs which inevitably follows from a salary system that has a strong bias towards seniority and corresponding annual wage increases. The government for its part had long campaigned to raise the age at which national pensions are payable (from sixty to sixty-five) and it was finally able to announce this important change in December 1993. These alterations to the politically sensitive pension law are to be introduced gradually until the minimum age for eligibility reaches sixty-five in 2013. Most firms are also moving to a higher retirement age for their more competent employees, while the government will be forced to raise pension and welfare contributions as the portion of the population nearing retirement age increases. No cabinet likes to increase taxes but, given the size of Japan's existing government deficit, it might be better to face the age problem sooner rather than later. The necessary funding for a greying society cannot be postponed indefinitely, though the vicissitudes facing public finance in the 1990s have made this unpopular task considerably more difficult. The bill for providing pension and medical care to a burgeoning portion of the Japanese people is not yet in. The present social security system is a complex amalgam of state and private components with low costs and high benefits in relation to national income. Obviously this will have to change as the demands on the pension funds escalate and the health burden grows, although attempts to increase contributions to governmental medical services have been resented by the public. It also dislikes the system whereby general practitioners appear on occasion to overcharge their patients, knowing that the insurance schemes will take care of inflated receipts. Reforms are needed but face powerful resistance from pressure groups. What is probably clear is that the social strains associated with an ageing population will be less than in western Europe. Far fewer Japanese grandparents are likely to be shunted off into old people's homes or geriatric ghettos on the warmer Pacific coast. Family obligations are still strong; age can have its rewards. It would raise few eyebrows if, for example, the LDP were to elect a new party president in his seventies rather than gamble with a younger figure in his fifties. Some distinguished industrial figures have been known to remain in harness into their eighties. Gerontocracy may not rule, but it can still subtly influence events from the sidelines. When in the winter of 1997 Prime Minister Hashimoto, for example, was faced with the issue of how to solve the recent financial crisis that saw the collapse of the first major Japanese commercial bank in half a century, he turned instinctively to former premiers Nakasone and Miyazawa for both advice and comfort.

Important economic and political change confronts today's Japan. Pessimists would claim that this is likely to create major tensions for the future, yet it might be safer to assume that these forces will not seriously disrupt the existing social structure. Identity shifts are taking place and the last two decades have witnessed what has been called an 'introspection boom', as readers eagerly bought up accounts that redefined their nation, but this need not imply accommodation will be impossible. A survey of some of the issues in the domestic sphere and with regard to foreign policy might be useful.

Much attention has been focused on the young. Youth is better educated (or at least stays on longer at school and university) but it can hardly be said to have rejected conservative values. Competition in high schools for the glittering prizes that admittance to a decent university can bring has not slackened off. The mushrooming of juku and the use of private tutors, deplorable as it may be for the very young, is testimony to the achievement orientation of many. The pressures on middle and high-school students have led many to espouse the cause of educational reform. Nakasone said it was one of his main objectives for 1984, not least because much of the increasing amount of juvenile delinquency has been attributed to educational factors. A decade later has seen Ozawa Ichiro arguing that 'the seeds of autonomy and subjectivity in Japanese children are discouraged from developing under the current education system'. Ozawa fears that the present arrangements 'cannot produce autonomous citizens' and that contemporary Japanese society 'lacks freedom'. In his view the nation requires strenuous education reforms to correct this deficiency. Vandalism and assaults are attributed to those who do less well in school. The issue of delinquency gets reams of attention in the press and on television, but it often appears relatively mild in comparison with the behaviour of teenagers in some European and American cities. Certainly by the time most students reach university there does not appear to be much anger in evidence. Students are generally apolitical. Japanese youth to date has retained one great advantage over its counterparts in Europe. Employment opportunities have remained generally good during a period that is seeing the highest European dole figures since the 1930s. This has contributed to the present retreat to privatism and political apathy. Having to hold down a job, while conforming to most family and company norms, means that youth is hardly about to change the status quo.

The problems of education are inevitably linked to the reconsideration of the role of women in Japanese society. Women take their twin tasks of mother and housewife most seriously, but with the size of families decreasing and the time necessary to maintain a small apartment or house diminishing many wish to find other outlets as their families grow up. Japanese men have not been particularly sympathetic. Single women can find jobs, though not often careers, but the choices for married women when they try to rejoin the labour force are restricted. The entire structure of companies would have to be rethought if women were to be regarded as possessing equal rights. Men would (and do) resist supervision by women. Few Japanese banks have appointed female branch managers. As recently as December 1983 the LDP selected only one woman to run in the forthcoming general election and, with the exception of the JCP, the other parties were equally timid. The era when Ms Doi Takako could be elected the first female leader of a major Japanese political party in 1989 has not been followed up by similar showings in rival parties. The so-called 'Doi boom' proved to be short-lived and did little to arrest what has by 1998 become the seemingly terminal decline of the Socialists. The present Hashimoto coalition cabinet does not have a single female minister.

No fundamental reconsideration of what women might wish to do with their lives is yet likely. Their opportunities have obviously grown in comparison with the restricted choices of their grandmothers but the traditional 'good wife and wise mother' ideal has a hollow sound to many young women. Marriage is frequently seen as something that might either be postponed until later or even avoided entirely. Yet it would take at least a generation for women to make any substantial inroads into the company hierarchies, assuming some were able to get a foot on to the career escalator. Within the existing family the great attention that mothers give their offspring has both had an immensely beneficial influence on the children's development and created psychological difficulties. Fathers, as we have seen, often leave the responsibility of bringing up children to wives, knowing only too well that many housewives dismissively employ the popular remark that 'the best husband is a healthy one who's never home'. All this may create too strong a bond between the mother and her young, which she may consciously or unconsciously promote. The result has been a legacy of overdependence for some, which leaves the child disappointed when his or her wishes and desire for affection are responded to less frequently or less intently later.

Until recently one commonly shared source of pride for many Japanese has been the growth of its economy. A decade ago the public had become sufficiently accustomed to substantial annual increases in Gross Domestic Product that the press instinctively referred to predictions of 4 per cent growth for the mid-1980s as 'low'. Slight it may have been to those who could recall the double-digit years, but when most advanced industrial nations were only emerging from the worst period of economic depression since the 1930s, the adjective was a comment on the extent of Japanese expectations. Japanese economic success did lead, not surprisingly, to greater self-confidence in its leaders and people, but the days of 'GNP-ism' appear to be over. In the 1980s this may have presented something of a dilemma for those concerned with Japan's future, yet the era when the Japanese economy was seen as an automatic gold medal winner is now little more than a fond memory. Even then, it should be noted, novel goals for a prosperous Japan were not put forward as alternatives to growth but rather as supplements to it. Prime Minister Nakasone could, therefore, in the course of his election campaign in December 1983 claim that he was 'trying to turn Japan into a country of peace and politics and culture – an international state'. The reference to culture, by which he presumably meant most forms of leisure activity from the cultivation of sports and hobbies to more serious intellectual endeavours, was a theme that the premier had used frequently in policy statements to the Diet. It was based on the premise of continued economic achievement. Nakasone's call at the beginning of his first term in office for 'a country of resilient culture and leisure' was intended to increase communitarianism and reevaluate the post-war reforms, while warning the public that 'even though Japan may be said to be better off than most countries, we face immediate problems in the economy'. No room for slackers was the message. If all rowed together, however, the public was assured by its political leaders that Japan would become what Nakasone's successors now term a 'lifestyle superpower'.

The subject of Japanese identity is one dear to the hearts of many Japanese. It is likely to remain a most imprecise quest, with opportunities for seemingly endless discussion on where Japan is and where it ought to be going. Some would argue that Japan's post-war history might be seen as an attempt to reconsider where the nation went wrong and how it might better behave with new values. The more sceptical observer might well respond to this type of argument by noting how little Japan had changed in reality. The debate is certain to continue. We might draw up a rough balance sheet to assess the relative strengths of the forces of change and the counter-pressure of continuity.

Our account of Japan's experience from 1945 to 1998 has suggested that much of the forced change imposed on Japan during the occupation years has persisted. Parts have undoubtedly been rejected and other portions modified better to fit Japanese circumstances, but large sections of the occupation's handiwork still exist. Should retired junior officials from the United States Government Section or the Labour Division of SCAP revisit Japan they would find little difficulty in recognizing parts of their legacy.

There may well have been pre-war precedents for parliamentary democracy or trades unionism, but the impetus from the Allies to strengthen what by 1945 were no more than latent elements in a wartime polity based on quite separate values should not be forgotten. Similarly the constitutional provisions with respect to Japan's defence and foreign policies have not been scrapped. Japan today can hardly be described as a military threat to the security of the Pacific. If its foreign policy appears weak-kneed we might remind ourselves that it has few sanctions that it can impose in order to gain its objectives. Of how many nation-states now in the United Nations can it be said that they have not fired a shot in anger since 1945? Precious few. The belief that Japan ought to continue to behave in accordance with the 1947 constitution is strong. Public opinion can be relied on for the remainder of the 1990s and probably beyond to oppose measures that some ministers might wish to implement to increase substantially Japan's defence capabilities. This may not be popular with the Pentagon but it will be greeted with relief by those Asians who recall the Japanese wartime occupiers and their reigns of terror.

Tokyo, however, can be rebuked for not breaking out of its chrysalis to approach the rest of the world except largely on the economic level. Japan's perceptions may be changing but until the evidence of this is apparent judgement has to be reserved on any real change of heart. The globe is still seen as a market for Japanese finished goods and a source of raw materials. This is a continuation of pre-war industrial policy. 'Export or Die' and 'Buy Japanese' are unstated slogans deeply embedded in the popular consciousness. Even today imported manufactured goods rarely make a substantial dent in Japan's balance of trade surplus and inward investment by foreign corporations is minuscule in comparison with the amounts Japan sinks into both developed and developing nations. Europeans, no doubt, ought to try harder, but Japanese spokesmen have a habit of gliding over their government's earlier trade policies that aided the growth of nascent industries. It would be surprising if Japan's bureaucrats and industrialists were readily to alter their instinctive response to promote exports when the domestic economy faces a mild recession. There is yet to be much action, as opposed to reaction, to overseas threats of protectionism, that takes note of the consequences of trading successes. At present the government encourages export drives rather than risk stimulating the domestic economy. Monetary and fiscal measures that might result in still larger government debt and higher taxes are held in reserve. The possibility of renewed trade friction at the turn of the century cannot be ignored, particularly when requests from other Asian states and the USA for Japan to boost its domestic economy are disregarded on the grounds of public indebtedness. The announcement in February 1998 that Japan's current account surplus had risen 60 per cent in 1997 led US Treasury Secretary Robert Rubin to warn of 'alarming trends' in international trade, but it is unlikely on past evidence that such warnings will lead to a change in Japanese policy.

Japan's rapid economic advances since the war have now reached the stage where it has overtaken nearly all of its competitors by most international comparisons. Certainly its economy has matured and there is anxiety, as one parliamentary vice minister acknowledged in January 1998, to gain 'the restoration of confidence in ourselves', but Japan's fifty years of success deserves to be given its due. Critics will insist that the result has been no more than an empty affluence, yet this is too harsh a judgement. Many British and Australian politicians would dearly love to be able to campaign on a record even half as impressive as that of Japan. In the 1970s and 1980s Japan generally had the highest average Gross Domestic Product growth rate, lowest inflation and, perhaps most topical of all, the lowest unemployment statistics of the advanced industrialized economies. Even in 1998 it has impressive currency reserves and a most successful manufacturing sector. The process of modernization embarked on over a century ago is obviously over. Some commentators would go so far as to suggest that Japan, having completed its 'catch-up' period, was until recently out on its own with the ability to show the way to other industrial societies. Be that as it may, a nation that has rarely had on average 3 per cent of its work-force laid off between 1952 and 1998 deserves to be taken seriously by contemporary historians and social scientists.

Such achievements were not easily gained and industrialization in Japan, as elsewhere, has caused disruption and hardship. Fishing villages and coal-mining towns lost their raison d'être. Farmers sold out to developers. Families became separated as sons went to work on assembly lines in Aichi and Kanagawa prefectures. Yet hard graft was accepted, for there appeared to be few alternatives. Inadequate housing, cold factories and cramped trains had to be tolerated if conditions might improve later. They did, though Western images have often not yet caught up with the more recent boosts in living standards. Yet it might be equally dangerous to swing to the other pole and imagine that the days of the work ethic are numbered. The competitive nature of Japanese society, reinforced by the strictures of parents, makes this improbable. Some relaxation has occurred and productivity in certain offices and public corporations, as opposed to industrial plants, may make officials despair of the future. But if the manner in which Japan overcame the disruptions of the twin oil shocks is any guide, it would be premature to start writing Japan off.

A nation's identity, its pattern of thought and behaviour, changes more slowly than shifts in economic development or institutional reform. Japanese values have gradually altered over the five post-war decades but the stress on homogeneity at the national and societal level has persisted. To give a few examples. Knowledge that Japan has overtaken the West (by some yardsticks at least) is one useful rallying cry. Tanaka Kakuei, when running as premier, used to stress the strength of the Yen against the dollar; Nakasone could hardly adopt that tactic but he would argue that 'before I became prime minister, Japan was pushed into a corner by others. Now the voice of Japan is being raised.' In the 1990s Ozawa Ichiro would write that 'in the realm of economic statistics, Japan is today running even with or even surpassing America' and that Japan's 'safety and stability are unmatched anywhere'. It is popular both to note Japan's economic progress and to argue that the nation is under threat from external forces. Nationalism is strong and the remainder of the world is seen, in that telling Japanese expression, to 'misunderstand' Japan.

Can one anticipate any diminution of this insularity?

Japan's post-war advances have given many the opportunity to visit other nations, albeit in often very restricted fashion under the restraints of time and the propensity to travel in groups on Japanese carriers, but how much difference this may have made to popular perceptions is unclear. Group tours to Asian capitals may confirm existing prejudices and even strengthen a sense of racial superiority. Reactions to visits to the West can be more complex. Europe may be merely a cultural museum for some and the United States a warning of the consequences of encouraging multiculturalism, yet others might return to question the economic priorities of Japan. More important than placing any hopes on tourism would be to encourage greater contact on the personal level. Educational exchange has hardly been attempted and will remain rare until the structure and attitudes of the academic and administrative staff of Japanese universities begin to alter. It is certainly the case that Japanese industry, under the pressure of the market, has been obliged to confront the world in a more determined manner than Japanese higher education has dreamt of. Yet a sense of difference and separateness is still at the heart of the Japanese identity. The nation, the family, the company, the school all recognize this and find it a far from deplorable state of affairs.

Social anthropologists and psychologists have cautioned the layman against using the term 'national character'. They, no doubt, have excellent professional reasons for warning us off, but historians are obliged to generalize if they want to be read at all and, so long as Japanese of quite disparate backgrounds and accomplishments continue to preface their remarks with reference to their shared identity, it will be tempting to assume that there are important cultural traits and, perhaps, certain personality types that predominate. It has already been suggested that one aspect of contemporary Japanese identity has been widespread involvement in groups that will make considerable demands on their members. A willingness to submerge one's own point of view in return for the protection and psychological security that membership will provide is common, as is also a wariness towards other potentially hostile groups. Political parties have their factions, university departments their opposing cliques and rival sections in trading companies may drink in different bars. All this may well contribute to the larger 'us' and 'them' pattern of much Japanese thinking towards non-Japanese.

What other patterns of behaviour are encouraged in Japanese society? Conformity, loyalty, deference, moderation in presenting one's own views and an acceptance of eventual decisions that are necessarily a compromise based on a rough consensus are all frequently claimed to be praiseworthy. No one seriously pretends that the realities of Japanese society correspond more than very approximately to these ideals, but children are taught in primary school and later to think of their classmates, and new employees in corporations will receive pep talks on cooperation that they will have at least to endure politely. Harmony is a goal, however, that has to be constantly worked towards and the need to stress it so often suggests to some that it might easily go missing. Conflict certainly abounds but it has frequently to be submerged, since most individuals have little choice but to remain with their associates or face the unpleasantness and uncertainty of abdication and isolation. The invocation throughout contemporary Japan of the English phrases 'my way' and 'privacy' is more the expression of a wish than a common reality. Obligations still last a lifetime. The tensions involved in working closely in small groups with individuals whom one may dislike can be imagined and give rise to after-hours drinking bouts where one can speak one's mind more freely with less risk of offence being taken.

Solidarity is one side of the coin; the other is dissent. Any overseas traveller to Japan who has arrived at Narita Airport and been processed through what can only be described as a fortified encampment might quickly wonder if this was quite the harmonious nation he had heard and read so much about. Later inquiries on the planning delays for the New Tokyo International Airport might reinforce his doubts on the validity of claims for the efficiency and foresight of Japan's bureaucrats, particularly when he recalls the distance and time involved in reaching downtown Tokyo from an airport still hobbled with only one runway in use decades after its inception. Other examples can be cited to remind us that Japan too has its share of social problems. The streets of Japan's cities are safe, but this does not preclude a nasty underworld that supervises prostitution, gambling and protection rackets. Gangsters (*yakuza*) have ties also to the right-wing political fringe and have developed the clever habit of packing stockholders' meetings with their stouter members to prevent effective discussion of company business. The connivance of major corporations in this activity only perpetuates the fraud. Mutual trust is another Japanese attribute that can be challenged. It does not prevent the most detailed investigation of candidates' backgrounds before admittance to large enterprises or the habit of employing various dubious means to look into family registers and financial statements before the selection of marriage partners. Likewise, social and racial discrimination abounds. Burakumin and Koreans are at the bottom of the pile. Those of Korean ancestry, who have lived their entire lives in Japan, are ineligible for employment in most public schools or the bureaucracy. Only recently have non-Japanese become eligible for professorships in national universities but this has led predictably enough to virtually no foreign appointments. Japanese universities are among the most insular in the world. But dissatisfaction with the status quo need not express itself in any political act. Few of those earning low wages attempt collectively to improve their position; most suffer in silence rather than risk jeopardizing an already precarious existence. Rocking the boat is a dangerous venture. Morale in Japanese enterprises is often far from the fever pitch of accounts in the Western press, yet unionization is declining. The LDP may be less popular, but this has not particularly aided the opposition parties as the proportion of those claiming to have no party allegiance has increased and the turn-out has dropped substantially in the 1990s. (It is below the British level but still far higher than the poor response to American presidential elections.)

A look at popular culture should tell us something about contemporary Japanese behaviour. At the broadest level it is frequently a combination of watching television, playing *pachinko* and drinking with work-mates before braving the long train journey home. But, of course, it is often more than merely TV for the sedentary and the occasional practice at the local golf range for the active, since whole areas of Japan's cities are set aside as entertainment quarters catering for most tastes and budgets.

The Japanese play hard. Within yards of the subway exit at any of the downtown intersections are scores of coffee shops, noodle restaurant chains, video-games parlours, bars, discos and, slightly away from the main thoroughfares, the Turkish bathhouses (now diplomatically retitled 'soaplands') and 'love' hotels. The Western image of Tokyo after dark as peopled only by sybarites and the privileged few on expense accounts is fortunately erroneous. Unfettered by licensing laws and with limitless tolerance of noise, the areas are crowded from early evening until the last train leaves for the suburbs.

What conclusions can be drawn from this energy and din? Is it merely evidence of an affluent, mass society comparable in British terms to Soho, Blackpool and Piccadilly rolled into one? While there are similarities, such as the lingua franca of pop, the motorbike gangs and pub crawlers, there are also differences. Cramped and often distant Japanese housing discourages entertainment at home and explains the plethora of restaurants and the institution of the coffee shop that serves as a de facto office for salesmen, rendezvous and escape hole from the company round the corner. Housewives are rarely involved in their husbands' leisure activities. Company receptions and trips are for company employees only. Wives are expected to rule at home and usually have control of the purse for major family purchases and to dole out an allowance to their husbands. This division of labour leaves Japanese wives in a far stronger position than some might imagine from accounts in the Western press. There is undoubted discrimination against women at work – female graduates are often taken on as glorified tea girls – but once married the situation is more equitable. Husbands are permitted some freedom to roam after-hours yet have limited financial independence. The salaryman and his coterie can pay frequent visits to their favourite bar to relax from the tensions of the office or shop-floor, but at home they may be lesser breeds. Some fathers' contribution to family life is often little more than an occasional excursion with their children on either a Saturday afternoon or, more likely, a Sunday. The slowness with which Japanese enterprises have moved to eradicate Saturday morning trading (only in 1983 did banks finally agree to start closing, though by today the process has been greatly accelerated and the inconvenience of having neither banks nor post offices open is much regretted) deliberately restricts the time and attention that a father can devote to his family. Take away Saturday morning attendance and the company loses a not inconsiderable hold over its employees. Smaller enterprises have been particularly reluctant to reduce their working week on both economic and psychological grounds.

If and when a family does go out together, its choice of destination is likely to be back into the downtown centres rather than outwards to the less-crowded regions. This willingness to return to the urban shopping and entertainment districts is dictated partly by the attractions of the cities and partly by the distances required for families in the Tokyo or Osaka conurbations to escape their environment. Willingly or not, most fathers accompanying their families on Sundays are likely to head for the branches of the major department stores that are a feature of Japanese life without any Western counterpart. Here the customer is king, since the Japanese consumer expects and generally receives both value for money and a great deal of service from attentive salespeople. Department stores – the secular cathedrals of contemporary Japan – take themselves seriously in other ways. Many of the exhibitions to be found in any Japanese city are sponsored and presented in the exhibition halls of stores. Japan would be culturally the poorer without these expensive and important displays. The size of the attendance figures on any Sunday at an exhibition, for example, of Impressionist paintings is evidence of the widespread Japanese interest in Western art and a clue perhaps also to the enduring limits of its taste.

Japan is more a nation of spectators than participants in

the realm of sport. Although most schoolboys are reared on baseball, few play this or any other game once they have left high school. The inadequacy of many urban sports facilities and the demands of the company over both work and leisure hours necessarily curtail opportunities for many. Golf remains the select preserve of the upper bourgeoisie, though those who can rarely afford to pay green fees still practise at the driving ranges. The latest spectator sports boom in the 1990s has been in soccer, where the professional J-League has established a strong presence that has led to the emergence of the Japanese national team as a force in Asian football. The sports centres that do exist are a telling commentary on Japanese social priorities, since they have frequently been constructed by urban companies as profit-making outlets rather than as community projects open to local residents. Far more males elect to visit the nearest race-course (hopelessly crowded on Sundays and without bookmakers), baseball park or pro-wrestling hall than take up jogging or locate a convenient municipal swimming pool. All this suggests why Japan's performance at international sporting events has been a bitter disappointment to the nation. Only in judo, volleyball and some winter sports, as during the 1998 Nagano Olympic games, has Japan won much distinction. It would dearly like to do better.

Many of these strictures over both the limits to leisure time and the lack of appropriate facilities may gradually lose their force. Contrary to popular perceptions, the average number of hours worked in manufacturing industries in Japan is considerably lower than in Britain and the United States and only slightly higher than in Canada. The great differences that remain are over fully establishing the five-day week and the reluctance of many employees to use up their entitlement to paid holidays. Only when this begins to change can one expect to see major shifts in the time available for leisure activities. The company continues to come first in the view of many Japanese. There may be some weakening of such attitudes among the young but not too much ought to be read into this phenomenon. The same salaryman who this year rushes to the ski slopes at the first available opportunity may shortly be putting in unpaid overtime as he comes up for promotion. Competition within the same year's entrants in a large enterprise is often fierce and personal priorities do switch. For most Japanese males the company is their master, much as their mothers dominated their childhood and their wives will control their retirement years.

For housewives there would appear to be a greater variety of leisure activities on offer as the traditional feminine arts of the tea ceremony and flower arrangement face competition from culture centres and keep-fit classes. Once mothers have got their youngest child off to primary school they may have time on their hands before their husbands return home late in the evening. Parent-Teacher Associations, cooking schools and, increasingly, a part-time job help to fill the void. Japanese companies remain, however, reluctant to reemploy women who had worked before their marriage and most housewives who can find work are obliged to accept low wages in manufacturing or service industries. The lack of government-sponsored day-care centres and the consequent rise of dubious commercial 'baby hotels' is a further difficulty that faces young mothers who want to get back into the labour market. Greater use of female employees would require changes in management attitudes and alterations to Japan's labour laws that presently restrict the hours and conditions of employment. In April 1998 Mitsubishi Heavy Industries' graduate intake of 530 new recruits included only ten women. Japan's men continue to see their wives' place as the home. Traditional attitudes still persist and indeed are reinforced by pressure from parents and company managers. If the only job one can find is assumed to be little more than of a temporary nature before marriage then it is difficult to take work too seriously and thus the prejudices of the company are confirmed. Office Ladies (OLs) may certainly be better educated than ever before but there is a limit to the ways in which one can receive company guests or answer the telephone. Not surprisingly, such women with considerable free time and money (many will still be living totally rent-free with their parents) form a valuable market for sports-goods manufacturers, department stores and travel agencies.

There are other sides to Japanese culture that also deserve mention. Western publishers can only look with envy at the size of the market for books and journals. A best-seller means something many times larger than a print run of 5,000 copies for a successful British novel. The cheapness of Japanese publications and the rarity still of public libraries contribute to the boosting of sales, as does the publicity associated with the nomination of titles for prestigious annual book awards. What do the Japanese read? The answer is a mixture of serious journals, glossy magazines, economic studies, 'How To...' books on professional, social and sexual issues and an endless range of lurid comics (*manga*). Comics, not just the province of children, account for a quarter of the books and magazines published. Translations of Western literature and current affairs also proliferate. Works on American management techniques are seemingly assured of success, as are foreign descriptions of the current Japanese scene, provided, perhaps understandably, that they are sufficiently laudatory. Praise from Western sources is always welcome and can produce the slightly absurd situation of

Japanese journalists reporting from Washington or New York the moment any front page story or magazine cover article appears, regardless of its content. Likewise, American television reportage from Tokyo or Kyoto to New York is instantly shown on Japanese screens, however trite or sensational it may be.

The two contemporary Japanese art forms best known to the West are the cinema and literature. Names such as Kurosawa Akira, Ozu Yasujiro and Mishima Yukio possess a sure niche, with retrospective surveys of post-war Japanese film being shown periodically in European and North American centres and translations of Mishima's works readily available in paperback. The Japanese cinema is deservedly accorded a great deal of respect. Kurosawa's films *Rashomon* and *Kagemusha*, separated in the making by thirty years, found popularity with two generations of audiences. Ozu's slow-moving accounts of the difficulties of Japanese family life have also had a considerable following abroad and there are some critics who have predicted a revival in the current fortunes of the Japanese cinema. Works, for example, by Oshima Nagisa have gained a certain notoriety in Europe, though the prudishness of Japan's censors has resulted in only stunted versions of his recent films being shown in his homeland. Most films made in Japan are less ambitious. The popular cinema continues to churn out the equivalent of pulp fiction with sentimental accounts of rural Japan, gangster movies, animated cartoons and vehicles for pop stars. There may presently, however, be something of a revival underway in more serious Japanese films; directors such as the late Itami Juzo and Kitano Takeshi have had success overseas as well as at home.

Mishima Yukio is undoubtedly the post-war Japanese writer best known to foreign readers. This has been through a combination of his literary merit and the flamboyance of his personality. His suicide in November 1970 was an international *cause célèbre*. It also greatly increased interest in Mishima's earlier publications and the final volume of *The Sea of Fertility* tetralogy that Mishima completed shortly before his death. Critics were quick to praise the work, while deploring the ultra-nationalism behind his foredoomed attempt to arouse Japan from what he saw as its materialism and opportunism. Countless theories were instantly minted to account for Mishima's action. The Japanese premier told the press that Mishima must have been mad. Others preferred to see the suicide as that of an ageing homosexual who felt his best work was now behind him and whose obsession with death was manifest.

One of Mishima's earliest literary sponsors was the writer Kawabata Yasunari, who in 1968 was to become the first Japanese author to gain the Nobel Prize for literature. Many have consistently maintained that either Tanizaki Junichiro or Mishima might have been a more appropriate choice. Tanizaki, who died in 1965, had written during the Pacific war an immensely long and involved family saga entitled *Sasame Yuki* (*The Makioka Sisters* was the English title) that has a vibrance lacking in Kawabata's more melancholy fiction. A visually fine film version of *Sasame Yuki* was made in 1983 by Ichikawa Kon, best known in the West for his film of the Tokyo Olympics. It is a commentary on European interest in Japanese culture that when Kawabata's Nobel Prize was announced none of his works were then in print in English. Happily this situation has since been rectified. His most popular works have been the early short story *The Izu Dancer* and the novella *Snow Country*. Both have retained their popularity through being made and remade in stage and film versions. Younger generations, however, are likely to be impatient with the themes and heroines of Kawabata and Tanizaki and turn instead to the likes of Oe Kenzaburo, who won the Nobel Prize in 1994, and Abe Kobo for works of more contemporary relevance. Among current writers Murakami Ryu, Murakami Haruki and Yoshimoto Banana have gained considerable followings; all three draw heavily on pop culture. *Coin Locker Babies*, for example, by Murakami Ryu is a hellish description of a Japan dominated by intrusive television stations, rock groups and mindless violence. In this episodic novel, one of the orphans of the title expresses the nausea of the times in the remark 'for Hashi, the idea that music could express human emotions was bullshit; in fact, the whole idea of human emotions made him feel a bit queasy'.

Yet music, Murakami's imagination aside, is the one art form to have achieved widest acceptance in its Western guise. The number and quality of orchestras in Japan testify to music's popularity. Tokyo supports a plethora of orchestras, as well as ballet and opera groups of high standing. Concerts by conductors of the calibre of Gerd Albrecht or visiting companies with the *cachet* of the Royal Ballet are certain to be sold out. Japan's musical exports to the West include the Suzuki method for training young violinists, the Yamaha piano and the dreaded karaoke. Theatre on the other hand has had a harder time of it. The language barrier immediately comes into force to restrict any potential audience. There is also competition from Japanese experimental drama and the classical *noh* and kabuki theatre forms which continue to have their bands of loyal followers.

Exponents in other fields where Japan has gained international recognition deserve to be at least mentioned. Modern architecture might be represented by Tange Kenzo and Ando Tadao, as witnessed by their overseas commissions, fashion by Yamamoto Kansai, Issey Miyake and Mori Hanae and Japanese food (and presentation) by its sushi masters. Japan has also a large number of talented photographers, illustrators and graphic designers whose careers have prospered in tandem with the growth of the Japanese advertising industry. It is perhaps appropriate that Japan's rapid post-war development has led to it boasting of the world's largest advertising agency. Despite the nation's artistic achievements and their influence on contemporary life, Japan in the last resort holds uncritically to a business culture. Its values look fated to remain those of the mass consumer society.

6

Malaise: contemporary Japan

I cannot possibly abandon reforms midway through.

Hashimoto Ryutaro, 1997

Some day we will all look back on the 1990–1997 period with incredulity and disbelief. Did a great nation really let itself flounder needlessly for so long. And all will ask: How can we ensure that this will never happen again?

Paul Samuelson, October 1997

Japan matters. Its considerable achievements since 1945 deserve to be better known overseas and its importance to the international community needs to be underlined both to the Japanese public and to outsiders. We must now prepare an approximate balance sheet on what Japan has accomplished in the past half century and assess the results for the nation, its neighbours and the wider world.

Perspective is all. Writing in the mid-1980s it was difficult not to recognize the heroic scale of Japan's post-war endeavours; fifteen years on it is impossible to maintain the same enthusiasm. In the interim Japan has disappointed its friends abroad by failing to strenuously reform its political, bureaucratic and corporate structures and by stumbling badly in the economic stakes where it had once appeared to be the all-conquering champion.

Since it was industrial prowess that first brought the nation back into prominence after the disgrace of defeat, it is hardly surprising that both Japan and the world continue to think instinctively of economic might when reassessing its reputation. There is no doubt, of course, that the contrast between the blitzed cities and hungry citizenry of the immediate post-war years and the new urban centres and affluent consumers of today is both stark and comforting. The western Tokyo suburb of Shinjuku in 1945 was literally rubble supporting merely a delapidated, wooden station. Fifty years on the area hosts the city's imposing municipal offices in a complex designed by Tange Kenzo. Tokyo's City Hall stands surrounded by hotels, corporate headquarters and a railway station where at the peak of the morning rush hour commuters in their tens of thousands stand patiently waiting for the order to line up on the appropriate platform. These same office workers enjoy a standard of living that was unimaginable at the end of the Pacific war and one that remained still improbable for all but the elite until recently. Today the urban commuter feels that his or her opportunities for self advancement and for leisure are comparable generally to those shared by their counterparts in the West. Salaries are high, the state provides decent health and pension systems and a degree of either satisfaction with, or at least acceptance of, the status quo is evident in election results and opinion polls. This is not to suggest that Japan is approaching human perfection in its contemporary form but it is a reminder of both the distance the nation has travelled since the Pacific war and the rewards that have become more widely distributed within society.

Yet there are most certainly faults in the manner in which

Japan organizes itself today. Housing policies for the Shin-juku commuters appear incapable of substantial improvement. The arrangements whereby land is kept off the market and the zoning densities of suburbia are maintained at low levels both contribute to an ever more distant search for affordable building plots. This has not deterred the ambitious, however, and Tokyo continues to be the magnet for the aspiring young, much as it has been since the Meiji period. The aim to own one's home and to be able to afford at least some creature comforts in old age motivates the middle classes, who instil the work ethic into their young. The youth of Japan knows from an early age that society is highly competitive and the less successful go to the wall. While inequalities are not approaching the glaring levels of the United States and Britain, the view that society has responsibilities to help the unfortunate is less accepted today. Groups without political influence are experiencing hardship and this trend will probably grow as the economy deteriorates.

In the last decade there has been considerable demoralization among white-collar workers, who thought that once they had demonstrated their commitment to the workplace their futures were secure until retirement. This is no longer the case. There have been severe dislocations in the 1990s to familiar post-war employment patterns. More and more companies are rethinking their recruitment policies with the result that even prestigious corporations are less prepared to offer the incentives of the past when male graduates from some select universities were hired in a seller's market. There is now a willingness to admit that the costs of the traditional corporate-style welfare system have become prohibitive. Market forces dictate that fewer graduate recruits will be taken on each spring and that more temporary staff should be employed if and when business fluctuations prompt their services.

As long as Japan's financial problems remain unsolved, it is difficult to see how the economy can easily revive. The full page advertisements in the English-language press that the Japanese government placed in February 1998 appeared widely optimistic when it was suggested that Japan will gain a stronger economy 'as surely as day follows night'. Two factors mitigate against an early improvement in Japan's financial and economic woes. First, the general level of household consumption continues to fall, though given the traditional frugality of many citizens at a time of widespread anxiety this is hardly surprising. Second, the weaknesses of many banks to maintain adequate borrowing/lending ratios have led to a very unpleasant credit squeeze for all but preferential clients. Until the public is persuaded that it is safe to splash out on major expenditures once again, it will be up to the government to decide whether it wishes to spend its way out of what is now a recession in all but official parlance. Ministerial and bureaucratic concern that this would postpone the badly needed improvement in Japan's huge public debt has had to be balanced against the fears of business and banks that there may be no alternative, if the economy is ever to turn the corner. Prime Minister Hashimoto, however, appears to wish both to kick start the faltering economy and to respect pledges to reduce the state's financial deficit. The world beyond Japan is certain to continue to complain at Tokyo's reluctance to stimulate domestic growth.

Any serious expectations that the proposed substantial reforms to Japan's governmental and economic systems might in themselves be sufficient to liberate and envigorate the nation's fortunes have faded. The belief that deregulation alone might be able miraculously to refloat the ship of state is now widely derided. The difficulties facing Japan appear almost impossible to solve until the banking sector is back in safe hands, but this will require a very different approach by government officials and financiers that is not at present visible. Any comprehensive series of reforms would necessarily require extensive deregulation, transparency, honest bookkeeping, the breaking of cosy ties between the public and private sectors and above all else a determination to let the banks alone to succeed or fail. In 1998 the Hashimoto coalition cabinet feels, however, that there must be no further disruptions and that public funds should be employed to shore up rather than alter the existing structure. Public opinion remains divided over whether this temporary arrangement is necessary or desirable, particularly as the media are carrying daily accounts of the incompetence and dishonesty of Ministry of Finance officials in their supposed role of bank supervision. By committing itself to safeguarding all major financial institutions, the government is, of course, permitting those felt to have incompetent management to escape censure. Reform appears a distant goal under the weight of pressing circumstances.

The Shinjuku commuter is incensed at the present banking fiasco and deeply resents the evidence of chicanery and corruption in public life. His confidence in the bureaucracy of Japan has clearly decreased as more revelations emerge of the extent of close cooperation between officialdom and business groups. The extensive use of 'parachuting', whereby senior civil servants acquire fresh posts after retirement in the very financial institutions that they had formerly been supervising and controlling, is a source of particular disquiet and deserves to be scrapped. If present disillusionment at the state's misbehaviour were to grow this would inevitably rebound on the head of both Mr Hashimoto and the LDP. Many urban Japanese already regard politicians across the spectrum with almost limitless cynicism and have shown in the 1990s that they are prepared to exact punishment either by voting down the conservatives or by simply crying a plague on all political parties and then registering their protest by refusing to vote. Given the doubts about the willingness of the LDP to implement political reform that would weaken substantially its ability to raise funds or to introduce strict anticorruption laws against the interconnected political, bureaucratic and corporate structure, the consequences could yet be severe for the conservatives. Events since the late 1980s in Japan have shown that crony capitalism is not merely a southeast Asian tradition; the difference in the case of Japan is that the electorate can throw out the ruling party for failing to pass an ethics bill or prevaricating over ministerial links to banks that are slow to report mountains of uncollectable debts.

With this barrage of bad news to digest, it is hardly surprising that issues involving the longer-term future are easily pushed to one side in Japan. Yet, as in other industrialized societies, there is some awareness that demographic changes will contribute to a harsher taxation system and place additional human burdens on many women in Japanese society. By 2020 it has been estimated that approximately twenty-six million citizens will be over sixty-five years old and this group would then comprise 18.8 per cent of the nation's population. The demands are likely to be heaviest on middle-aged females, who will be asked to take care of elderly parents or parents-in-law, while looking after their own families. The alternative of greatly enhancing the state's provision of sheltered accommodation and special homes is seen as both expensive and going against the grain of close family involvement with the aged.

Japan is equally hesitant to alter firmly entrenched positions over foreign policy. The public and parts of the bureaucracy see little advantage in assuming wider responsibilities in international affairs. This is particularly the case with current Japan, where the strains of coping with its own domestic financial difficulties are narrowing horizons and making it harder for politicians to propose greater assistance to the ailing economies of Thailand and Indonesia. The rhetoric of a decade ago when Japan boasted about appointing itself the leader of Asia for what was then being heralded as the Pacific Century has largely vanished.

Consideration of how Tokyo would handle its future relations with the People's Republic of China if there were crises over the Korean peninsula, the Taiwan Straits or any repetition of the Tiananmen Square massacre are generally left undiscussed. The dangers of unpreparedness are reckoned to be less pressing than the risks involved in engaging in an open debate that would inevitably disrupt Japan's diplomatic ties with its neighbours. It is precisely this large area of uncertainty that the United States as Japan's only military ally is endeavouring to persuade Tokyo to address. Recent consultations between the US and Japanese governments have gone some way to establish guidelines on what roles the Japanese SDF might be called upon to perform, if there were a large-scale emergency in northeast Asia.

A similar reluctance to clarify in detail the nature of Japan's responsibilities is evident in its long-standing bid for a permanent seat on the UN Security Council. Despite assurances from senior UN officials that Japan's constitutional prohibitions over the use of force would not inhibit its ability to become a member of the Council, doubts persist over what exactly Tokyo might be expected to contribute to the effectiveness of the institution. Japanese public opinion appears to regard the gaining of a seat more as a trophy that the nation has deservedly earned through its financial support for the UN than the occasion for demonstrating international maturity and leadership. It is hard at present to envisage any possible return to the unprecedented efforts that Japan made in assisting the UN during the Cambodian transitional period. Public opinion remains uneasy about even the remotest prospect of putting the lives of Japanese military and civilian personnel at risk and does not take much notice of entreaties to consider the wider issues in play. In the case of the Cambodian intervention, the Miyazawa cabinet would have fallen if there had been a single additional Japanese casualty. The new UN-centred interventionism of the post-Cold War era is not about to become a Japanese burden sharing exercise.

The world remains for Japan something that has to be confronted largely on the economic front. Given that domestic immigration is discouraged, minorities face discrimination and multiculturalism is seen as highly disruptive, it inevitably follows that Japanese society rarely meets or converses with non-Japanese at home. It is only after leaving Narita that it becomes necessary to step outside the circle and experience differing realities. Tourism, however, probably does rather little to alter public attitudes, since those returning from abroad usually note the cheapness of prices overseas rather than question why identical products may be more expensive within Japan. It is not free-spending tourists in Los Angeles and Rome but Japan's businessmen and traders stationed abroad who have put Japan on the map. These individuals are responsible for the successes of Japanese goods, financial services and factories overseas. They are, in the military metaphors beloved of older corporate leaders, the shock troops who first established the beachheads and then eventually built Japan's permanent bases across the globe. Major Japanese trading houses, for example, have a ring of offices and agents on all five continents that provide detailed day by day financial and political information and analysis for their headquarters in Tokyo and Osaka. (Final decisions are almost invariably the responsibility of management teams back in Japan.) Such institutions pride themselves on the range and sophistication of their activities and regard themselves as very much the commercial representatives of the nation overseas. In the same manner, the largest Japanese manufacturing corporations also take their responsibilities abroad seriously, knowing full well that the human and economic impact, for example, of a Sony plant in south Wales or a Kikoman food factory in the American mid-west on the local community can be intense. The corporate strategies of companies the size of Sony are designed to have sufficiently diversified global operations so that mishaps in any one region will not substantially affect total earnings. Thus when the southeast Asian economies are in difficulties, a company of the calibre of Toyota should be able to shift resources to expand its sales in Latin America to take advantage of the growing Brazilian and Argentinian markets. The successes of this new Japanese economic empire have clearly demonstrated that the nation has been able to build an infinitely more resilient, larger and fairer system than its ramshackle and grossly inhumane wartime co-prosperity sphere.

Japan is and will remain for the foreseeable future an economic superpower. Statistics released in the spring of 1998 show that the nation is once again enlarging its trade surpluses with the rest of the world and that in the case of the politically sensitive bilateral balance with the United States, Japan had in 1997 a trade surplus of $55.687 billion, almost exactly half the total of the US's entire international deficit. Clearly it is impossible for the rest of the world to ignore Japan's presence as an immense exporter and investor, though the current domestic apprehensions over the country's immediate and long-term prospects appear certain to persist into the next century. Editorials in the Japanese press warn of negative factors that are now eroding Japan's international competitiveness and thus the affluence that has come to be taken for granted by younger people. It will be difficult, however, to regain easily even portions of this lost vitality, given the resistance to effective deregulation and structural reform now evident. The ambivalence of the governing party over streamlining the bureaucracy and confronting the pain that would necessarily accompany innovation suggests that only a major crisis could prompt the sea change in attitudes and policies that were seen in Britain in the 1980s under Mrs Thatcher. In place of reform, the ruling LDP-led coalition government continues to hope against hope that economic recovery will somehow miraculously emerge and thereby defeat these persistent calls for radical thinking and new policies.

Japan remains reluctant both to adequately confront its pre-surrender history or to accept that harsh measures are called for to prepare the way for a future where the comforts and delights of the present might be better maintained. It prefers rather to view the last fifty years as a self-contained unit that will yet provide an adequate recipe for its progress in the twenty-first century. This complacency is both dangerous and myopic. The Japanese state and people are running out of ideas that will shape the future to their own ends. The rest of Asia in the last generation has scuppered the propagandists' claims of the uniqueness of the Japanese economic accomplishments, while the United States has demonstrated that its own house-cleaning measures have arrested its economic decline and shown Japan that it once again needs to learn from America. We should be hearing much less from now on about the economic invincibility of Japan and the intellectual challenges that the Japanese public policy model holds for the West.

Learning certainly needs to become more of a two-way street for many in Europe and North America, but it would be the height of arrogance for Japan to ignore the contributions of its main benefactor and protector on the post-war road to democracy and prosperity. To imagine, as many appear to do despite knowledge of their nation's desperate circumstances after 1945, that the Japanese 'miracle' was exclusively made in Japan is a travesty of history. It was the calculated benevolence of the United States that laid the foundations for reconstruction, though, of course, no amount of foreign loans and technological transfers would have been of much use without the ability of Japanese corporate managements and their workforces to utilize this aid in a highly effective manner. Equally, the creation of the post-war liberal international trading system by Washington would have been largely irrelevant if Japan had not quickly developed a range of manufactured exports that could find ready markets overseas. Similarly, the United States' perception of Japan as a vital geopolitical factor in the Cold War in Asia from the outbreak of the Korean war onwards greatly boosted Japan's strategic importance and led to the crafting of highly favourable and non-punitive peace settlements. Throughout the Cold War decades Japan was also spared the need to make any substantial security commitments that would have delayed the concerted efforts of state and people to modernize at such extraordinary speed.

The West was generally surprised by this great leap

forward and uncomfortable with what little it was told of the collaborative, semi-planned nature of the Japanese experience during the two critical decades of hypergrowth from the mid-1950s to the mid-1970s. The result was that the solid industrial and financial foundations of post-war Japan were securely in place long before voices in the United States began to call for retaliatory measures to safeguard American jobs. By then Japan had created a robust economy out of most inauspicious and divided beginnings that in turn helped form the social stability that endures to the present. This is not to ignore the fierce political differences of the immediate post-surrender years or the security crisis of 1960 but to emphasize that even during the moments of greatest upheaval and mass protest there were only isolated instances of resorting to the pre-war habit of drawing the assassin's sword. Violence from left or right has been rare; the military has remained in barracks.

While Japan continues to take justifiable pride in its relatively safe streets and consistently low crime rates, disappointment at the nation's paltry economic accomplishments over the past decade is unmistakable. It will have to get used to more headlines in the West that speak of 'the wilted chrysanthemum' and reckon with critical calls for more innovative policies to end the slump. Instead of responding to the challenges of change, however, the response of Japan in the 1990s has been to rely instinctively on the type of arrangements that worked so well a generation ago. The return of the LDP to power has strengthened the government-industry links that were once central to Japanese modernization. In addition, the slowing down of the economy has further increased the influence of officialdom in attempting to take care of the many threatened financial institutions and in protecting the small and medium-size industries that are still the backbone of the manufacturing sector.

The past is probably an unhelpful model for Japan in the next century. The arrangements of the 1950s and 1960s were designed to gain rapid and unfettered national economic growth under highly difficult circumstances, but to persist in a set of arrangements that still cossets entire industries and reduces the competitive winds that rage beyond Japan will lead almost certainly to eventual failure. The public has little inkling yet of what price may have to be paid for persisting in protective measures that are unlikely to do much but postpone rather than solve pressing problems. The banking sector is receiving vast sums of public money to shore up quite indiscriminately both competent and insolvent institutions. Similarly, the construction industry has been set the task of lavishly rebuilding the nation's schools, hospitals and roads, very largely in order to maintain present employment levels. In the western Tokyo suburb of Ogikubo virtually every public building from high school to sports centre has been knocked down recently and then rebuilt; it would have been far better if the money had been spent on improving the still poor standard of the area's housing stock.

There remain doubts too over the extent to which the political system can be said to have been reformed. There have indeed been efforts recently to correct the electoral system, as we have seen, but though politics in contemporary Japan is certainly pluralistic and interest groups are free to compete for legislation and policies favourable to their goals, the behaviour of individual politicians and parties has often been a source of major domestic criticism. Yet important academic works on Japanese democracy appear willing to overlook a great deal of decidedly shabby dealing that permits collusion between politicians, the bureaucracy and industry. The expense of running in elections is still huge, although the state underwrites some of the costs, but this is hardly an adequate defence for the succession of almost daily scandals that emerge. (In fact, the word scandal is a misnomer as no one in Japan is the slightest bit shocked by yet more revelations of bribery and favouritism.) The public too deserves to be included in this criticism, since in many constituencies politicians are judged by their ability to provide construction projects galore; pork barrel successes are the basis for reelection in large areas of the country. Given the prevalence of such attitudes, Japanese politics remains locked in a dismal localism that the LDP has effectively exploited by stressing time and again at general elections that it alone has the experience and clout to win the budgetary debates and force the ministries to allocate funds for pet projects.

The future course of Japanese politics appears unlikely to alter these seemingly enduring traits. Prime ministers come and go, cabinets are reshuffled almost on a seasonal basis and the opposition's political parties are presently following a confusing process of fragmentation and relabelling. The system has a decidedly weak ministerial structure that often is under the sway of permanent civil servants, and the picture is further complicated by decentralized and factiona-lized political parties. Given such arrangements, the bureaucracy may not formally be king but it certainly knows how to rule. In its defence it has to be said that no alternative decision-making body has a fraction of its skills and exper-tise, though this hardly justifies the lack of constraints on the far ranging authority that the mandarins possess and readily deploy. Administrative guidance leaves a great deal of power in the hands of the bureaucracy, which also prospers through the public's criticism of the nation's politicians.

Although Prime Minister Hashimoto has vowed to initiate sweeping reforms of the political system, it is most unlikely that he has either the power base or the individual determination to combat the inevitable howls from his opponents that this would provoke. As a professional politician, who has spent his career working closely with officials, he knows that their cooperation and goodwill are required for cabinets to succeed. Instead of working to loosen the substantial role of the bureaucrats, he would prefer to do no more than chastise them over instances of widely reported misbehaviour. Prime Minister Hosokawa, by way of contrast, enjoyed complaining of how, during his years as governor of Kumamoto prefecture, he could not even order a change in the siting of a bus stop without the permission of the ministry of transportation in Tokyo. The public at large likes to applaud these attacks on the bureaucracy, and with good reason given the revelations of the Ministry of Finance's failing to supervise the banking sector, but it would be lost without them. Ever since the Meiji state was constructed on the basis of a strong, centralized bureaucracy, the officials organizing and at times directing affairs have been seen as the central force in the land. There is no substitute. It would take a radically different political culture to alter the powers of the bureaucracy and to devise a governmental system whereby the prime minister, his cabinet and the majority party could confidently and competently determine how Japan be run.

To gain even consideration of such a scheme, it is necessary to look to the opposition to the LDP. The conservatives themselves are too inhibited through ideology, personal connections and the sizeable recruitment of ex-bureaucrats who win election to parliament to contemplate substantial change. Yet the frequent and confusing temporary realignments and subsequent splinterings among centralist parties suggest that administrative reform will not occur in the foreseeable future. It is this inability of opposition groupings to explain clearly where they stand and what they intend to do if they gain office that severely dampens the hopes of anti-LDP voters. Disillusionment is made worse by the manner in which some politicians will break ranks with the conservatives in order to curry favour with the electorate, but after joining an opposition party will suddenly slink back to reenlist in the old guard. Only when there is greater clarity and cohesion among the opponents of the LDP will the public entrust government to these new parties. At present they serve more as a vehicle for collecting the votes of the dissatisfied than a force for change. The opportunity would appear to exist for an effective, united anti-LDP movement, since recent opinion polls reveal that over half the electorate has no political affiliation, yet little has been accomplished. The conservatives remain highly unpopular but the opposition is nowhere. The creation, however, in March 1998 of a four-party merger under the Democratic Party of Japan's banner with Hosokawa Morihiro and Hatoyama Yukio as its leaders may help increase the opposition's influence in the immediate future against a numerically superior Liberal Democratic Party.

The conservatives face two hurdles in their bid to be accepted once more as the permanent government of Japan. The first and most obvious difficulty that the party has not solved is the continuing weaknesses of several important areas of the Japanese economy. Fortunately for the nation, manufacturing corporations have demonstrated generally more resolve than the protected financial and distribution sectors. Toyota, for example, has been able to weather the storm by a series of management changes and cost reductions that suggest that the future for the Japanese car industry, with the possible exception of the faltering Mazda company in Hiroshima where Ford is back in control, is once again bright. Yet Japan is about to go into recession. Although government spokesmen are reluctant to admit what the Shinjuku commuter can see instinctively through his own corporation's sales figures and the comments from his family about cutting back on personal expenditure, few doubt this reality. The question that the LDP-led coalition cabinet prefers to duck is what emergency fiscal measures might be introduced in the near future to prevent a further worsening of the situation. Unfortunately the issue of attempting to reduce the massive national debt is regarded by the financial bureaucrats as more pressing than the need to prevent a further downturn in the economy that would also hurt the rest of the world. The Asian economies are certain to suffer from such damaging Japanese policies and so too will the United States as the rest of the Asian-Pacific region attempts through currency devaluations to export its way out of its current financial problems.

The second hurdle that the LDP has constantly to guard against is the prospect of another party split. It was, it will be recalled, precisely the inability of the conservatives to placate the Ozawa group that led first to intraparty warfare, then to the fracturing of the party and on inevitably to the loss of office in 1993. The expectation of Mr Ozawa and his faction that their apostasy would 'create a political system supported by two major parties under which a change of regime can take place' has proved to be only half true. This long predicted move did temporarily leave the LDP out in the cold, but in 1998 the hopes of Ozawa that he could ride to power on the back of an anti-LDP monolithic party have been dashed. By the spring of 1998 Ozawa was left leading a Liberal Party of only fifty-three Dietmen. The opposition appears to be presently in a far worse condition than even the most optimistic of LDP strategists could have anticipated prior to the October 1996 general election. The constant reshuffling among these groups continues. In March 1998, for example, the creation of an expanded Democratic Party of Japan, probably under the eventual leadership of the popular figure of Kan Naoto, may have difficulty agreeing on policy goals. Kan warned that the bureaucracy was enjoying too much power and called for a 'revolution' to offset officialdom's controls but there appears to be little but rhetoric to the Democratic Party's realignment. Its best hopes of toppling the conservatives depend on the formation of a stable centre-left coalition alliance.

It appears probable that, provided the LDP can maintain some subtle mixture of discipline and camaraderie and immediately set about the task of restoring the economy, it may yet be forgiven for past greed and mistakes. The determination of the LDP to draw on its lengthy experience of power to avoid any return to its short but humiliating years in opposition may bind the party together. It was also assisted by the recent electoral reforms that make it probable that the LDP, as the only truly national party in Japan, can dominate the 300 single-seat constituencies and thus leave the smaller opposition parties to divide up only the crumbs collected from the remaining 200 proportional representation seats. The conservatives presently find themselves in a more fortunate position than they objectively deserve on the strength of their recent record. Contemporary Japan does not appear to be much nearer the old dream of an alternating two-party parliamentary system.

7

Prospects: future challenges

Of course, Japan is making progress in shouldering its global political responsibilities. But in the years ahead there must be greater harmonization of burdens, responsibilities, and powers for maintaining the peace and stability from which Japan benefits.

Morita Akio, 1993

Japan today seems to be in its twilight, and there are no dreams for the future of the country.

Kato Koichi, October 1997

Japan at century's end is a chastened nation. Its confidence in its exceptionalism has been eroded by a series of jolts to its economic and psychological well being during the 1990s. It remains a nation with very considerable assets but it faces a range of domestic and international issues where neither the state nor the public appears well prepared for what may be unpleasant choices. There remains both a great deal of unfinished business in the area of political, administrative and educational reform and a considerable gap between what other powers regard as responsible action towards the wider world and what Tokyo still sees as excessive and unreasonable demands.

The present decade has left Japan aware of serious

economic and social faults at home. Less than a generation earlier the nation had been able to take legitimate pride in its impressive economic and financial successes, but by 1998 there could be no disguising the change in the way Japanese and outsiders view Japan. It has to be said that a number of what today are seen as widely held criticisms of the Japanese way of conducting business or mollycodling its entire financial sector were tolerated then without particular comment. What had changed by the late 1990s was public anger that large sums from its pocket have had to be employed to buttress a system that remains doubly protected from both overseas competition, though this either has changed or will do shortly, and by ministerial guidance within Japan. Equally, the frequently predicted improvement in the general state of the economy has simply not occurred. Despite government statements and private sector announcements, the new realities of wage reductions and job losses are unavoidable even to a society that is in the habit of curtailing reference to bad news. Should there be further substantial rises in the number of unemployed then the social fabric would be tested as it has not been since the dark days of Japan's immediate post-war era, though the state can be relied upon to do everything within its powers to avoid this prospect. What has to date prevented any marked deterioration in job losses, despite the severe economic climate, has been the reluctance of employers to take such drastic steps and thereby damage morale within their companies and destroy their reputation in any future competitive labour market. How long this unofficial truce can endure will soon be known as many small and medium-size enterprises face a credit squeeze from their own bankers, who are in turn under pressure to call in loans to present a more favourable picture of the financial sector. Under such circumstances the role of government can only grow as it will be expected both to guarantee the safety of bank deposits and to extend low interest bearing loans to industry.

For the moment Japan continues to enjoy a degree of social stability that has few parallels in other nations. The fairly equal distribution of income levels, at least in the first post-war generation when much of the population was equally poor, and the fact that unemployment rates remain low even today perhaps acount for portions of this remark-able phenomenon. The remainder may be the consequence of the extreme homogeneity of Japanese society where cul-tural patterns and educational standards are reasonably uniform, though it certainly helps to go to high school in an affluent Japanese suburb rather than a country school in Niigata prefecture and to be blessed with middle-class parents who have ambitions for their offspring. The fact that most citizens apparently identify themselves as positioned somewhere in the loosely defined middle classes is also useful in cementing society together. In truth, contemporary Japan is probably less equal than some claim, but as long as many persist in holding to such self-imagery then this myth presumably works to avoid dissension. Clearly the class, religious and ethnic divides of Japan remain much weaker than in what it regards as less fortunate and more polarized nations.

Yet contemporary Japan must now confront the question: 'What has gone wrong?' Whether it is journalists asking the head of a MITI think tank why Japanese corporations are less productive and less competitive than their overseas rivals or housewives anxious about a possible run on their local bank, the need is to tackle what Prime Minister Hashimoto has been forced to call 'systemic fatigue'. There is indeed talk of the 'Japanese disease' and however imprecise the phrase may be, it does reflect the widespread sense of unease readily apparent today. Since the present coalition cabinet appears to be unable to take sufficiently bold action to lift public morale, it is likely that the current air of indecision will continue. The only two ways forward may be for the LDP either to select a fresh leader of the calibre of Kato Koichi, the party's secretary-general, or to soldier on with the present arrangements until after the next general election, assuming that this more risky strategy might be able to secure a stable majority for the conservatives.

Regardless of the political climate, some estimate as to the length of time required to correct Japan's faults is called for. Mr Hashimoto would have us believe that 1998 will be the year 'for overcoming the final phase of the postbubble period', but the present deterioration in the economy is such that few take this recent policy statement to the Diet too seriously. The alternative view, shared by senior officials in the Clinton administration, is that the Japanese government is failing to correct its economic and financial position by rejecting calls from abroad to boost domestic demand. The consequences for the rest of Asia, and indeed the global economy, could be severe if Tokyo chooses to avoid substantial tax cuts at a time when an estimated 20 million jobs in the region are likely to have been lost by 1999 as a result of the financial instability that began in Thailand and then spread to much of southeast Asia and South Korea.

In the short and medium term future, it is highly unlikely that the Japanese economy can rebound to refute the many critics of government fiscal policy. The first clear indication of an improvement in economic prospects will be seen through a raising of the extraordinarily low interest rates (savers are presently offered such derisory terms that bank deposits are hardly more attractive or necessarily much safer than storing cash at home) and a correction in the Yen:dollar foreign exchange rate mechanism. Yet it may be two years before some modest economic growth is in evidence and many observers expect little improvement thereafter until consumer confidence is firmly restored, particularly as the vital American market cannot be safely assumed to continue at its present enviable rate of growth much beyond 1999. Sceptics are entitled to reserve judgement on the future progress of the Japanese economy, given the large number of false dawns that have confounded many reputable forecasters since the early 1990s. The depth and longevity of this decade's woes will not be quickly forgotten, particularly as Japan is having to witness the successes of both the United States and Canada in balancing their budgets and to sit through foreign lectures on how best Tokyo should act to stimulate growth.

Demoralization and disillusionment at home feed incessantly off the present economic weaknesses of Japan. The nation discovers more faults with its government and officials as it asks itself what has gone wrong, in much the same way as, in a more extreme case, the British have had to endure decades of similar doubts over their own institutions. It is hard though to hear very much debate on what might be the most appropriate road to recovery other than by following in the wake of authority, since the public expects the state to regulate, control and offer directions on what is best for Japan and its people. Unemployment may be at its highest since 1953, and the weaknesses of the economy apparent in the Bank of Japan's extraordinary 0.5 per cent discount rate, but few alternatives to existing policies are evident.

Even when the economy eventually improves, Japan has still to ask itself what its next goals should be. Yet prime ministerial policy statements in the 1990s have rarely done much to point the way, since they are invariably the work of bureaucrats and contain little that reflects the personality of the speakers. Mr Hashimoto has spoken of the duty of politicians to chart the future, but in terms of content he falls back on platitudinous expressions on individualism and creativity. Similar imprecision exists elsewhere. Mr Ozawa, for example, has called for Japan to revert to a more ordinary form of behaviour that would see the partial abandonment of its post-war mentality. Yet when tackled in public over the concrete details of this bid to rework Japan as a 'normal nation', Ozawa's programme appears less radical. In foreign policy his schemes would not greatly ease Japan out of its continuing caution and his care before the last general election to invoke 'the spirit of the Constitution' was intended to reassure his uneasy supporters that Japan would not join in collective self-defence activities. Equally, it is hard to even imagine a Japan that was serious about a state that voluntarily stood back and encouraged autonomy for its citizens, corporations and communities. Ozawa is surely correct to plead for some relaxation in the regulatory powers of officialdom but neither the bureaucracy nor the public would take kindly to any such drastic reforms. Japan is still the complete nanny state. Society prefers to voluntarily submit to intrusions and interference in exchange for protection and security. It is an implicit bargain that has served both sides well in the past but will be increasingly difficult to sustain as the global economy and its market mechanisms penetrate more thoroughly into more areas of Japanese life.

It is also apparent that contemporary Japan has yet to discover fully how to balance the pleas for internationalization that were first heard in earnest during the Nakasone years with the wishes of many that the nation stand by to repel all boarders. The pressure from outsiders to persuade Japan to reconsider its narrow obsession with economism is certain to continue; cynics will say that change is best achieved when foreign voices echo the aspirations of reformers within Japan. Trade liberalization, issues of women's rights and responsibilities for refugees have gained fresh converts since the 1980s through this dual diplomacy. Most of this overseas pressure has come from the United States and the European Union. Since Japan sees itself as in permanent competition with the West and enjoyed, at least until the 1990s, proclaiming that it had first caught up with and then overtaken the United States and the sluggish Europeans, its perceptions of its Asian neighbours are generally a mixture of patronization and ignorance. If the popular belief is half true that 'Japan knows everything about America, while America knows nothing about Japan', it may also be that the adage can be adapted and that 'South Korea knows everything about Japan, while Japan knows nothing about South Korea'. Equally, students in southeast Asia often share a far greater knowledge of contemporary Japan than their counterparts in Tokyo and Osaka possess of ASEAN or its member states. Fortunately, there is evidence that this may be changing as Japan appears serious over moving closer to the region in order to develop political and cultural links that might eventually supplement the existing economic and financial ties. It remains to be seen, however, whether this is just a passing fad or if the so-called 'tilt' towards Asia reflects substantial changes in the post-Cold War international environment. How the Japanese government responds to the current financial turmoil in east and southeast Asia is clearly the region's most pressing concern. It will certainly test the commitment of the Japanese state and its major corporations to stay the course and reveal more on Prime Minister

Hashimoto's claims to be running a broader, proactive foreign policy.

Japan faces the twenty-first century with less of the confidence that it enjoyed merely a decade ago. Belief in the efficacy of its state and the performance of its economy has shrunk, while social concerns over the education and behaviour of the youth of Japan have further dampened most remaining optimism on prospects for the nation's future. The need to find solutions to these pressing issues requires that Japan stop congratulating itself both on having overtaken the West and for serving as a role model to others in Asia and to better concentrate instead on repairing the damage to its economy and social fabric. The need surely is not to invent new technological frontiers but to address more prosaic questions on how to reform Japan's public life and to begin to move the state out of areas where the bureaucracy has long been supreme. For many Japanese this will prove to be unpleasant medicine, and it is far from certain whether any future government, however large its majority, would be prepared to introduce more than superficial change.

Japan's post-war history is gradually ending. The long established patterns and policies for state and people are losing their validity as newer realities at home and abroad impinge on the nation. This erosion, however, is unwelcome to those many groups and individuals who flourished under a system that preferred to leave unquestioned the automatic priority on growth and the wisdom of the higher bureaucracy. Yet the experiences of the 1990s are a warning to Japan that economism has its high price and that complementary values need to be considered. Any critical review of Japan's experience since the humiliations of defeat, surrender and occupation, must fully acknowledge the nation's past successes and then ask whether its post-war history is now proving more of a hindrance than a help in confronting the future. Since it is unlikely that a mature Japanese economy can ever regain more than a fraction of its earlier vitality or that contemporary society would willingly submit to the constraints and privations of an earlier generation, now may be the moment to encourage broader goals. Japan's chairmanship of the Kyoto climate conference in December 1997 and its co-sponsorship of the UN resolution over Iraq in March 1998 are recent examples of the government's preparedness to begin to speak up on international issues; further measures to assist the southeast Asian economies would reinforce this trend.

Eventually the economy will rebound. Yet this long-awaited and still unsighted recovery is unlikely to restore lost Japanese pride in full or signal any repetition of the frenetic behaviour of the late 1980s. Tokyo now has finally to accept that other Asian states are more likely to grow faster than itself and that China, in particular, may in the next generation become both an economic superpower and a new political rival. Japan, however, should be able to flourish through continuing its global inward investment strategies and by its skills in converting advanced technological research into new consumer products. The repatriation of profits and dividends earned abroad is expected to be sufficient to ensure the nation's prosperity, as it confronts the costs of welfare and pension payments to its ageing population. Yet both the Japanese state and its people must avoid the great illusion of imagining that past achievements and present benign international realities will automatically continue uncontested into the future. Decline should not be seen as merely the fate of others. It can happen here.

APPENDIX 1

Prime Ministers of Japan, 1946–98

May	1946(a)	Yoshida Shigeru	Dec.	1978	Ohira Masayoshi
May	1947	Katayama Tetsu	July	1980	Suzuki Zenko
Mar.	1948	Ashida Hitoshi	Nov.	1982	Nakasone Yasuhiro
Oct.	1948	Yoshida Shigeru	Nov.	1987	Takeshita Noboru
Dec.	1954	Hatoyama Ichiro	June	1989	Uno Sosuke
Dec.	1956	Ishibashi Tanzan	Aug.	1989	Kaifu Toshiki
Feb.	1957	Kishi Nobusuke	Nov.	1991	Miyazawa Kiichi
July	1960	Ikeda Hayato	Aug.	1993	Hosokawa Morihiro
Nov.	1964	Sato Eisaku	Apr.	1994	Hata Tsutomu
July	1972	Tanaka Kakuei	June	1994	Murayama Tomiichi
Dec.	1974	Miki Takeo	Jan.	1996	Hashimoto Ryutaro
Dec.	1976	Fukuda Takeo	July	1998	Obuchi Keizo

(a) Date of initial Cabinet formation

Prime Minister Hashimoto finally resigned in July 1998 to accept responsibility for the dismal showing of the LDP in the summer Upper House elections. His party was trounced by its inability to solve Japan's continuing economic and financial problems. The conservatives then selected Obuchi Keizo as their new leader. As prime minister he faces the near intractable task of reinvigorating the economy without first sorting out the vast indebtedness of the banking system or insisting on comprehensive reform of the politically-sensitive bureaucratic and industrial sectors. The appointment of Miyazawa Kiichi as finance minister may hold out some hope of confounding Japan's many critics at home and abroad, but it is difficult to see much prospect of substantial change. The fear that further Yen depreciation may lead to major regional currency realignments and instability throughout Asia has intensified.

APPENDIX 2

Chronology of post-war Japanese history

Post-war Shōwa period (1945–89)

1945	Allied occupation of Japan begins
1946	A new constitution is promulgated
	The SCAP-sponsored land reform law goes into effect
1948–9	The Dodge line – economic stabilization ordered
1949	Nobel Prize in physics to Dr Yukawa Hideki
1951	San Francisco peace treaty
	Concurrent signing of mutual security agreement with the United States
1952	Japan regains independence
1953	Television broadcasting begins
1955	Japan Productivity Centre is organized
	Economic Planning Agency is formed
	Japan Socialist Party formed through merger
	Liberal Democratic Party formed through merger
1956	Restoration of diplomatic relations with USSR
	Japan's admission to the United Nations
1957	Completion of the nuclear reactor at Tokaimura
1958	Undersea Shimonoseki-Moji tunnel is completed
1959	Marriage of crown prince with a commoner

1960	New US-Japan mutual security treaty concluded amid demonstrations
	'Plan to double individual's income' is initiated
1964	New bullet train between Tokyo and Osaka opens
	Tokyo Olympics
1967	Rapprochement with South Korea following Prime Minister Sato's visit
1968	Yawata and Fuji are merged to form New Japan Steel
	Nobel Prize in literature to Kawabata Yasunari
1969	Student activists occupy Tokyo University
1970	Japan signs nuclear nonproliferation treaty
	Expo '70 opens in Osaka
1971	Merger of Kangyō and Daiichi, making it the largest bank in Japan
	Environment Agency established
1972	Winter Olympics open in Sapporo
	Okinawa formally returned to Japan
	Normalization of relations with Beijing
1973–4	The first oil crisis
1974	President Ford visits Japan, first visit by a sitting American president
	Sato Eisaku receives Nobel Peace Prize
1975	The bullet train is extended to Hakata in Kyushu
	Emperor Hirohito visits the United States
1976	The Lockheed bribery scandal implicating former Prime Minister Tanaka
	Narita International Airport (Tokyo) opens
	Life expectancy exceeds that of Sweden
	Japan-China treaty of friendship is signed
1979	The Tokyo summit of advanced industrial nations
1980	Japanese automobile production exceeds that of America
1981	Voluntary restriction of car exports at 1.68 million units to the United States

	Administrative reform movement is spearheaded by Doko Toshio, former president of Keidanren

Administrative reform movement is spearheaded by
Doko Toshio, former president of Keidanren
1982   Northeast bullet train line opens to Morioka
Bullet train line reaches Niigata on the Japan sea coast
1983   National debt reaches 100 trillion Yen
Tokyo Disneyland opens
1985   The Plaza accord to deflate the value of the dollar
against the Japanese Yen
Equal employment opportunity law for men and
women enacted
1987   The Japan National Railway is made into seven
separate private companies
Crisis in stock market (20 October) an average of 14.9
per cent loss in price in one day
1988   Opening of the Hokkaido-Honshu tunnel
Opening of the Seto bridge linking Honshu and
Shikoku
General sales tax instituted, going into effect 1 April
1989
1989   Death of Emperor Hirohito and accession of Akihito

Heisei period (1989–   )

1989   The Recruit scandal forces the resignation of Prime
Minister Takeshita
LDP suffers its first major defeat in the House of
Councillors election (23 July)
1991   Japan pledges a total of $13 billion to the Gulf crisis
Severe stock market loss, disclosure of illegal refunds
by Nomura Securities
1992   Participation in UN sponsored peacekeeping
operations [PKO] approved
Emperor Akihito and Empress Michiko make their
first official visit to China
1993   End of LDP's consecutive one-party rule since 1955

	Trade surplus reaches $132.6 billion and US dollar hits the 100 Yen mark
1994	Modified single-seat constituency for the House of Representatives passes
	New Osaka international airport opens
	The New Frontier Party (NFP, Shinshinto) is formed
1995	The Kobe earthquake
	Poison gas attack on civilians in Tokyo subways by the Aum Shinrikyo sect
1996	Merger of Mitsubishi and Tokyo creates the largest bank in the world
	First election under modified single constituency election law
1997	LDP regain majority position in the lower house of the Diet
1998	Yen slips to 140 to the dollar; its lowest level in seven years

From David J. Lu, *Japan: A Documentary History*. Reproduced by permission.

APPENDIX 3

Security treaty between the United States and Japan, 8 September 1951

Japan has this day signed a Treaty of Peace with the Allied Powers. On the coming into force of that Treaty, Japan will not have the effective means to exercise its inherent right of self-defence because it has been disarmed. There is danger to Japan in this situation because irresponsible militarism has not yet been driven from the world. Therefore, Japan desires a Security Treaty with the United States of America to come into force simultaneously with the Treaty of Peace between the United States of America and Japan. The Treaty of Peace recognizes that Japan as a sovereign nation has the right to enter into collective security arrangements, and further, the Charter of the United Nations recognizes that all nations possess an inherent right of individual and collective self-defence.

In exercise of these rights, Japan desires, as a provisional arrangement for its defence, that the United States of America should maintain armed forces of its own in and about Japan so as to deter armed attack upon Japan.

The United States of America, in the interest of peace and security, is presently willing to maintain certain of its armed forces in and about Japan, in the expectation, however, that Japan will itself increasingly assume responsibility for its own defence against direct and indirect aggression, always avoiding any armament which could be an offensive threat or serve other than to promote peace and security in accordance with the purposes and principles of the United Nations Charter.

Security treaty between the United States and Japan

Accordingly, the two countries have agreed as follows:

Article I. Japan grants, and the United States of America accepts the right, upon the coming into force of the Treaty of Peace and of this Treaty, to dispose United States land, air, and sea forces in and about Japan. Such forces may be utilized to contribute to the maintenance of the international peace and security in the Far East and to the security of Japan against armed attack from without, including assistance given at the express request of the Japanese Government to put down large-scale internal riots and disturbances in Japan, caused through instigation or intervention by an outside Power or Powers.

Article II. During the exercise of the right referred to in Article I, Japan will not grant, without the prior consent of the United States of America, any bases or any rights, power, or authority whatsoever, in or relating to bases or the right of garrison or of maneuver, or transit of ground, air, or naval forces to any third Power.

Article III. The conditions which shall govern the disposition of armed forces of the United States of America in and about Japan shall be determined by administrative agreements between the two Governments.

Article IV. This Treaty shall expire whenever in the opinion of the Governments of the United States of America and of Japan there shall have come into force such United Nations arrangements or such alternative individual or collective security dispositions as will satisfactorily provide for the maintenance by the United Nations or otherwise of international peace and security in the Japan Area.

Article V. This Treaty shall be ratified by the United States of America and Japan and will come into force when instruments of ratification thereof have been exchanged by them at Washington.

IN WITNESS WHEREOF the undersigned plenipotentiaries have signed this Treaty.

DONE in duplicate at the city of San Francisco, in the English and Japanese languages, this eighth day of September, 1951.

APPENDIX 4

Treaty of mutual cooperation and security between the United States and Japan, signed at Washington, DC, 19 January 1960

The United States of America and Japan,

Desiring to strengthen the bonds of peace and friendship traditionally existing between them, and to uphold the principles of democracy, individual liberty, and the rule of law,

Desiring further to encourage closer economic cooperation between them and to promote conditions of economic stability and well-being in their countries,

Reaffirming their faith in the purposes and principles of the Charter of the United Nations, and their desire to live in peace with all peoples and all governments,

Recognizing that they have the inherent right of individual or collective self-defence as affirmed in the Charter of the United Nations,

Considering that they have a common concern in the maintenance of international peace and security in the Far East,

Having resolved to conclude a treaty of mutual cooperation and security,

Therefore agree as follows:

Article I. The Parties undertake, as set forth in the Charter of the United Nations, to settle any international disputes in which they may be involved by peaceful means in such a manner that international peace and security and justice are not endangered and to refrain in their international relations from the threat or use of force against the territorial integrity or political independence of any state, or in any other manner inconsistent with the purposes of the United Nations.

The Parties will endeavor in concert with other peace-loving countries to strengthen the United Nations so that its mission of maintaining international peace and security may be discharged more effectively.

Article II. The Parties will contribute toward the further development of peaceful and friendly international relations by strengthening their free institutions, by bringing about a better understanding of the principles upon which these institutions are founded, and by promoting conditions of stability and well-being. They seek to eliminate conflict in their international economic policies and will encourage economic collaboration between them.

Article III. The Parties, individually and in cooperation with each other, by means of continuous and effective self-help and mutual aid will maintain and develop, subject to their constitutional provisions, their capacities to resist armed attack.

Article IV. The Parties will consult together from time to time regarding the implementation of this Treaty, and, at the request of either Party, whenever the security of Japan or international peace and security in the Far East is threatened.

Article V. Each Party recognizes that an armed attack against either Party in the territories under the administration of Japan would be dangerous to its own peace and safety and declares that it would act to meet the common danger in accordance with its constitutional provisions and processes.

Any such armed attack and all measures taken as a result thereof shall be immediately reported to the Security Council of the United Nations in accordance with the provisions of Article 51 of the Charter. Such measures shall be terminated when the Security Council has taken the measures necessary to restore and maintain international peace and security.

Article VI. For the purpose of contributing to the security of Japan and the maintenance of international peace and security in the Far East, the United States of America is granted the use by its land, air, and naval forces of facilities and areas in Japan.

The use of these facilities and areas as well as the status of the United States armed forces in Japan shall be governed by a separate agreement, replacing the administrative Agreement under Article III of the Security Treaty between the United States of America and Japan, signed at Tokyo on February 28, 1952, as amended, and by such other arrangements as may be agreed upon.

Article VII. This Treaty does not affect and shall not be interpreted as affecting in any way the rights and obligations of the Parties under the Charter of the United Nations or the responsibility of the United Nations for the maintenance of international peace and security.

Article VIII. This Treaty shall be ratified by the United States of America and Japan in accordance with their respective constitutional processes and will enter into force on the date on which the instruments of ratification thereof have been exchanged by them in Tokyo.

Article IX. The Security Treaty between the United States of America and Japan signed at the city of San Francisco on September 8, 1951, shall expire upon the entering into force of this Treaty.

Article X. This Treaty shall remain in force until in the opinion of the Governments of the United States of America and Japan there shall have come into force such United Nations arrangements as will satisfactorily provide for the maintenance of international peace and security in the Japan area.

However, after the Treaty has been in force for ten years, either Party may give notice to the other party of its intention to terminate the Treaty, in which case the Treaty shall terminate one year after such notice has been given.

IN WITNESS WHEREOF the undersigned plenipotentiaries have signed this Treaty.

DONE in duplicate at Washington in the English and Japanese language, both equally authentic, this 19th day of January, 1960.

APPENDIX 5

Japan and its neighbours: military strength

Country	(a) Population (thousands)	(b) Size (thousand sq. km)	(c) Personnel (thousands)	(d) Reserve forces (thousands)	c/a	c/b	d/c	Defence expenditure as % of GDP
Japan	124,593	378	240	48	2.0	0.6	0.2	1.0
South Korea	44,908	99	633	4,550	14.1	6.4	7.1	3.8
North Korea	23,760	121	1,132	540	47.6	9.4	0.5	26.7
China	1,148,593	9,561	3,300	1,200+	2.9	0.3	0.4	3.2
Taiwan	21,265	36	360	1,653	16.9	10.0	4.6	5.4
US	251,843	9,373	1,914	1,784	7.6	0.2	0.9	5.1
Russia	148,041	17,750	2,720	3,000	18.4	0.2	1.1	N.A.

Source: Tomohisa Sakanaka, 'Political Upheavals Sharpen Japan's Security Debate', *Insight Japan*, 1995, vol. 3, no. 4, p. 6. Reproduced by kind permission *Insight Japan*

Notes: c/a = personnel per 1,000 population; c/b = personnel per 1,000 sq. km of territory; d/c = reserve members per active soldier; N.A. = not available

APPENDIX 6

Japan's economic and financial changes since 1988

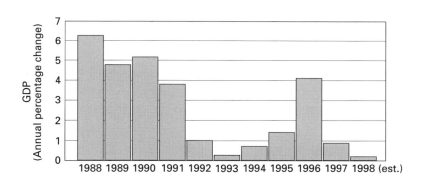

APPENDIX 7

Japan and international comparisons

	China	Japan	Germany	USA	Russia
GNP (1994, in billions)	$630.2	$4,321	$2,076	$6,737	$393
GNP per capita (1995)	$620	$39,640	$27,510	$26,980	$2,240
Human Development Index (1994, global rank)	108	7	19	24	67
Number of strategic nuclear warheads (1996)	275	none	none	8,111	6,758
Military expenditures (1995, in millions)	$31,731	$50,219	$41,815	$277,834	$82,010
Arms sales (1995, % of global total)	2	1	4	49	10
International currency reserves (1995, in millions)	$80,288	$192,620	$121,816	$175,996	$18,024

Official Development Assistance (1994, in millions)	($3,521)[1]	$14,489	$1,633	$7,367	($2,358)[2]
UN budget assessments (1995–1997, % of total)	.74	15.65	9.06	25.0	4.27
IMF voting power (1996, % of total)	2.28	5.54	5.54	17.78	0.26
World Bank voting power (1996, % of total)	2.03	10.76	6.97	14.98	0.26
Number of influential patents and global rank (1991)	n.r.[3]	76,984 (2)	17,749 (3)	104,541 (1)	n.r.[3]

[1] Amount received from donors, 1995

[2] Amount received from donors, 1994

[3] Not ranked among top 15 'patent powers'

Sources: United Nations Development Program; World Bank; World Resources Institute; Arms Control Association; IMF; Samuel S. Kim, *China In and Out of the Changing World Order* (Princeton: Center of International Studies, Princeton University, 1991)

APPENDIX 8

Japanese school system

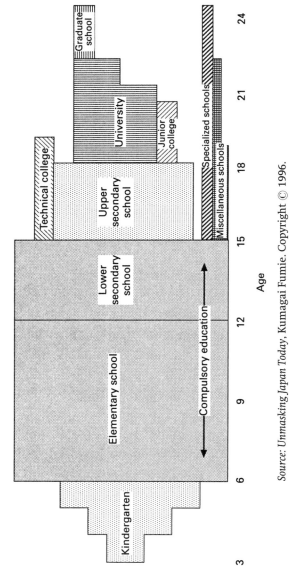

Source: Unmasking Japan Today, Kumagai Fumie. Copyright © 1996.
Reproduced with permission of Greenwood Publishing Group, Inc., Westport, CT.

APPENDIX 9

Changes in the proportion of the Japanese elderly by age group: 1930–2025

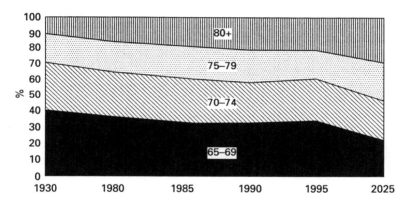

Source: Unmasking Japan Today. Copyright © 1996. Reproduced with permission of Greenwood Publishing Group, Inc., Westport, CT.

APPENDIX 10

Japanese party system, 1946–96

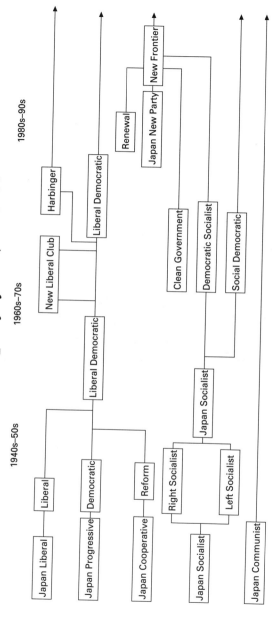

Source: Japanese Democracy, Bradley Richardson. Copyright © 1997.
Reproduced with permission of Yale University Press, New Haven, CT.

Bibliography

(Many of the works listed below are available in paperback.)

General Texts

Beasley, W. G., *The Rise of Modern Japan* (Tokyo, 1990)
Cambridge Enyclopedia of Japan (Cambridge, 1993)
Cortazzi, Hugh, *The Japanese Achievement* (London, 1990)
Kodansha Encyclopedia of Japan (Tokyo, 1983; supplement, Tokyo, 1986)
Reichauer, Edwin O., *The Japanese Today* (Cambridge, Mass., 1986)
Storry, G. R., *A History of Modern Japan* (Harmondsworth, 1978)

History

Armacost, Michael H., *Friends or Rivals?* (New York, 1996)
Buckley, Roger, *US-Japan Alliance Diplomacy, 1945–1990* (Cambridge, 1992)
Dower, John W., *Empire and Aftermath: Yoshida Shigeru and the Japanese Experience, 1878–1954* (Cambridge, Mass., 1979)
Eto Jun, *A Nation Reborn* (Tokyo, 1974)
Gordon, Andrew (ed.), *Postwar Japan as History* (Berkeley, 1993)
Ienaga Saburo, *The Pacific War* (New York, 1978)
Kano Tsutomi (ed.), *The Silent Power* (Tokyo, 1976)
Kawai Kazuo, *Japan's American Interlude* (Chicago, 1960)

Bibliography

Lee Chae-Jin, *Japan Faces China* (Baltimore, 1976)

Livingston, Jon, Moore, Joe and Oldfather, Felicia, *The Japan Reader 2, Postwar Japan: 1945 to the Present* (Harmondsworth, 1976)

Mendl, Wolf, *Japan's Asia Policy* (London, 1997)

Scalapino, Robert A. (ed.), *The Foreign Policy of Modern Japan* (Berkeley, 1977)

Ward, Robert, and Sakamoto Yoshikazu (eds.), *Democratizing Japan: the Allied Occupation* (Honolulu, 1987)

Welfield, John B., *An Empire in Eclipse* (London, 1988)

Wilkinson, Endymion, *Misunderstanding, Europe vs Japan* (Tokyo, 1981)

Yoshida Shigeru, *The Yoshida Memoirs* (London, 1961)

Politics

Baerwald, Hans H., *Party Politics in Japan* (Boston, 1986)

Calder, Kent E., *Crisis and Compensation* (Princeton, 1988)

Callon, Scott, *Divided Sun* (Stanford, Calif., 1995)

Curtis, Gerald L., *The Japanese Way of Politics* (New York, 1988)

Destler, I. M., Clapp, Priscilla, Sato Hideo and Fukui Haruhiro, *Managing an Alliance* (Washington, DC, 1976)

Inoguchi Takashi, *Japan's International Relations* (London, 1991)

Inoguchi Takashi and Okimoto, Daniel I. (eds.), *The Political Economy of Japan, Vol 2, The Changing International Context* (Stanford, Calif., 1989)

Johnson, Chalmers, *MITI and the Japanese Miracle* (Stanford, Calif., 1982)

Johnson, Chalmers, *Japan: Who Governs?* (New York, 1995)

Masumi Junnosuke, *Contemporary Politics in Japan* (Berkeley, 1995)

Ozawa Ichiro, *Blueprint for a New Japan* (Tokyo, 1994)

Newland, Kathleen (ed.), *The International Relations of Japan* (Basingstoke, 1990)

Richardson, Bradley, *Japanese Democracy* (New Haven, Conn., 1997)

Bibliography

Stockwin, J. A. A., *Japan: Divided Politics in a Growth Economy* (London, 1982)

Tanaka Kakuei, *Building a New Japan* (Tokyo, 1973)

Thayer, Nathaniel B., *How the Conservatives Rule Japan* (Princeton, 1969)

Yamamura Kozo and Yasuba Yasukuchi (eds.), *The Political Economy of Japan, Vol 1, The Domestic Transformation* (Stanford, Calif., 1987)

Economics

Abegglen, James C., and Stalk, George, Jr., *Kaisha, The Japanese Corporation* (Tokyo, 1987)

Austin, Lewis (ed.), *Japan: The Paradox of Progress* (New Haven, 1976)

Bergstein, C. Fred, and Cline, William R., *The United States-Japan Economic Problem* (Washington, DC, 1985)

Clark, Rodney, *The Japanese Company* (New Haven, 1979)

Cohen, Stephen D., *Uneasy Partnership: Competition and Conflict in US-Japanese Trade Relations* (Cambridge, Mass., 1985)

Denison, Edward F. and Chang, William K., *How Japan's Economy Grew So Fast* (Washington, DC, 1976)

Dore, Ronald, *Land Reform in Japan* (London, 1959)
British Factory-Japanese Factory (Berkeley, 1973)

Hanami Tadashi, *Labour Relations in Japan Today* (Tokyo, 1981)

Ito Takatoshi, *The Japanese Economy* (Cambridge, Mass., 1992)

Japan Institute for Social and Economic Affairs, *Japan 1998 – An International Comparison* (Tokyo, 1998)

Kitamura Hiroshi, *Choices for the Japanese Economy* (London, 1976)

Lincoln, Edward J., *Japan Facing Economic Maturity* (Washington, DC, 1988)

Minami Ryoshin, *The Economic Development of Japan* (Basingstoke, 1986)

Nakamura Takafusa, *The Postwar Japanese Economy* (Tokyo, 1983)

Okita Saburo, *Japan in the World Economy* (Tokyo, 1973)

Patrick, Hugh and Rosovsky, Henry (eds.,), *Asia's New Giant* (Washington, DC, 1976)

Tsuru Shigeto, *Japan's Capitalism* (Cambridge, 1993)

Yamamura Kozo (ed.) *Japan's Economic Structure: Should It Change?* (Seattle, 1990)

Culture and Society

Ben-Ari, Eyal, *Changing Japanese Suburbia* (London, 1991)

Bernstein, Gail, *Haruko's World: a Japanese Farm Woman and Her Community* (Stanford, Calif., 1983)

De Vos, George A., *Socialization for Achievement* (Berkeley, 1973)

Doi Takeo, *The Anatomy of Dependence* (Tokyo, 1973)

Fukutake Tadashi, *The Japanese Social Structure* (Tokyo, 1982)

Hendry, Joy, *Understanding Japanese Society* (London, 1987)

Hibbert, Howard (ed.), *Contemporary Japanese Literature* (Tokyo, 1978)

Kaplan, David E., and Dubro, Alex, *Yakuza* (London, 1987)

Kraus, Ellis S., Rohlen, Thomas P., and Steinhoff, Patricia G. (eds.), *Conflict in Japan* (Honolulu, 1984)

Kumagai Fumie, *Unmasking Japan Today* (Westport, Conn., 1996)

Mishima Yukio, *The Sea of Fertility, Tetralogy* (Tokyo, 1972–4)

Murakami Ryu, *Coin Locker Babies* (Tokyo, 1996)

Nakane Chie, *Japanese Society* (Berkeley, 1970)

Oe Kenzaburo, *A Personal Matter* (Tokyo, 1969)

Richie, Donald and Anderson, Joseph I., *The Japanese Film: Art and Industry* (Princeton, 1982)

Stronach, Bruce, *Beyond the Rising Sun: Nationalism in Contemporary Japan* (Westport, Conn., 1995)

Tsurumi Kazuko, *Social Change and the Individual* (Princeton, 1970)

Ueda Atsushi, *The Electric Geisha: Exploring Japan's Popular Culture* (Tokyo, 1994)

Upham, Frank, *Law and Social Change in Postwar Japan* (Cambridge, Mass., 1987)

Vogel, Ezra, *Japan as Number One* (Cambridge, Mass., 1979)

Index

Index

banks
  and economic recession 90–1,
    178, 186, 201
  employees 142, 154
  interest rates 195–6
  and manufacturing industries
    65
  Zaibatsu 21
Barshefsky, Charlene 104
bill of rights 13
birth rate 150
Blair, Prime Minister Tony 94
blue-collar workers 142
books 169, 170–1
bribery 138, 187
Britain 69–70, 125, 150, 167, 183
Burakumin 135, 163
bureaucracy
  and the economy 62, 70–1
  and Nakasone's premiership 40,
    48, 51
  need to reform 197, 199, 201
  public attitudes to 178–9
  strength of Japanese 5
  and Yoshida's premiership 31
  and the Zaibatsu 21
Bush, President George 126
business culture 173
business groups
  and trade unions 9
  weaknesses of 5
  Zaibatsu (pre-war industrial
    combines) 9, 20–1
businessmen, stationed abroad
    181–2

Cambodia 95, 132, 181
Canada 167
capital investment 80
capitalism in Japan 62, 83
car manufacturers 64, 74, 189–90

Carter, President Jimmy 123
Chiang Kai-shek 121
China
  comparisons with Japan 214–15
  future prospects 200
  and Japanese reconstruction
    21
  Japanese relations with 99, 100,
    102, 120–3, 128, 133, 180
  land reform 18
  military strength 212
  and the San Francisco
    conference (1952) 25
  and Tanaka's premiership 37
  US relations with 36, 106, 120,
    122–3
cinema 170
cities see urban environment
citizenship rights 136
City of London 50
class see social class
Clinton, President Bill 113, 126
coffee shops 165
Cold War 4–5, 23, 46, 56, 70, 75,
    94, 99, 101, 105, 184
  and Korea 123
comics 169
Communism
  and the Allied occupation 9, 10,
    23
  collapse of 99
  decline of 120
  and the LDP 56
  and nationalism 137
  and Yoshida's premiership
    30–1
  companies 140–5
  see also employment; industries
constitution
  Meiji 13, 15
  post-war (1947) 13–15, 98, 108

224

and Europe 124–7, 128, 131
and internationalism 77–8,
   128–9, 130–3, 197–200
and Korea 100, 102, 111–12,
   119, 123–4, 180
and the LDP 32–3, 34–6, 58
and Nakasone's premiership 40,
   41, 42–6
and Russia 117–20, 122
and the Socialists 58
and the United States 93, 94,
   95, 110–11, 112–17, 128
see also defence and security
   policy
foreign residents in Japan 135
France 69–70, 73, 126
Franco, General Francisco 9
Fujiwara Sakuya 134
Fukuda Takeo 36, 38

G-8 nations 92, 93
Galbraith, Kenneth 85–6
gangsters 163
GATT (General Agreement on
   Tariffs and Trade) 70, 124
Gaulle, Charles de 73
GDP (Gross Domestic Product)
   155, 159
Japan and international
   comparisons 214
Germany 28
comparisons with Japan 214–15
West Germany 81, 150
gifts, exchange of 138
global economy 4, 49–50, 104,
   106, 195
Japanese public opinion on
   107–8
GNP (Gross National Product),
   Japan and international
   comparisons 214

golf 167
government, post-war democratic
   reforms 12–15, 19
graduate employees 140–2, 165,
   176
grandparents 139, 151, 152
'Green Associations' 87
group norms, conformity to 138,
   162–3
Gulf War (1990–1) 132
Gunther, John 71–2

Harada Koichi 123
Hashimoto Ryutaro 2, 41–2, 60,
   94, 109, 113, 152, 174, 197
and the economy 177, 178,
   194–5, 201
and political reform 188
Hata Tsutomu 57
Hatoyama Ichiro 30, 31, 118
Hatoyama Yukio 189
health services 84, 87, 150, 151–2
Hendry, Joy 134
Higashikuni 29
Hirohito, Emperor
and the Allied occupation 7,
   16–17, 19
and US–Japan relations 93
death and funeral 54–5
Hiroshima 79, 88, 96, 125
history, teaching of Japanese 137
Hosokawa Morihiro 57, 58, 188,
   189
hospital care 84
hours of work 144
housewives 134, 154, 155, 165,
   168
housing 81, 82, 87, 88–9, 159, 165,
   176, 186
costs 83, 139–40
for employees 141

Index